Information
interviewing

How
to Tap
Your
Hidden Job
Market

2nd edition

Martha Stoodley

Library of Congress Cataloging-in-Publication Data
Stoodley, Martha.
    Information interviewing : how to tap your hidden job market / by Martha Stoodley.
        p.   cm.
    Includes bibliographical references.
    ISBN 0-89434-175-8
    1. Job hunting.   2. Interviewing.   I. Title.   II. Title:
    Information interviewing.
    HF5382.7.S763   1997   97-41267
    650.14--dc20   CIP

Published and Distributed by
J.G. Ferguson Publishing Company
200 West Madison Street, Suite 300
Chicago, IL 60606
(312) 580-5480

Printed in the United States of America
U-9

About The Author

Martha Stoodley began her career counseling work in 1967 as the manager of a temporary personnel agency in the Midwest. After moving to California, she earned a Bachelor's Degree in Psychology, and a Master's Degree in Educational Psychology/Clinical Counseling from California State University at Hayward, CA; she holds a Counseling License in California (MFCC) and a Lifetime Community College Teaching Credential. As a county agency coordinator, Martha helped women get back on their own by providing counseling and career advice. As a high tech recruiter for a corporation with 10,000 employees, she interviewed applicants for professional positions in engineering and management. In 1984, Martha began a career counseling private practice which evolved to include a training and consulting service. She was adjunct faculty at John F. Kennedy School of Professional Psychology in Campbell, CA, and facilitated seminars for the American Management Association. Martha's career development articles have appeared in newspapers and magazines.

Now the President of Stoodley & Associates, Martha works in an electronic cottage in San Jose, California. Stoodley & Associates is an international management consulting and education firm specializing in career development, communication, team learning, leadership, employee surveys, executive coaching, and employee education. Martha and her associates work with individuals, work groups and teams to improve their skills and productivity, but primarily to improve the quality of work life in any organization where they consult. Meaningful work is essential to her evolving career, and information interviews have played a significant role in finding ways to earn a living that provide enjoyment and satisfaction.

Acknowledgments

Thank you to the clients who stimulated my interest in the topic of information interviewing. Their frustration with gaining and conducting information interviews stimulated me to provide a step-by step, pragmatic resource for job seekers and career changers.

For the 1997 revision, several colleagues contributed their support. Gail Webber provided the current resources for the bibliography. Jean Perera did an excellent presentation of information for the chapter on Online research. Nancy Rodriguez helped with the word-processing, and took over some of my work so I could dedicate time to the book. Shelley Paris provided frequent encouragement and collegial friendship along the way. Bob Calvert at Garrett Park Press suggested the revision, complete with pep talks. Without them the work would have been less interesting and enjoyable. I'm grateful to them all.

Table of Contents

Introduction

It has been said that college students are often willing to work themselves into nervous exhaustion studying to achieve an A grade in a class that no one will ever know they took but are unwilling to go to the trouble it takes to explore and find a satisfying career path and then vigorously pursue a job in that field.

Indeed, most of us wish we could take a career planning class or hire a consultant or go to a psychic who would tell us what we should do. We don't want to take all the time and effort required to find out for ourselves.

Too often that approach results in spending years doing work for which we aren't suited. More than 80 percent of Americans would like to change their jobs. That is reason enough to take a long hard look at what's available before you build a lifetime of experience in work you don't like. A recent newspaper article on an engineering manager who walked out of his job quoted him as saying, "Never become too good at something you hate. They'll make you do it the rest of your life." His co-workers envied his walking out so much, they developed a cult that celebrated his actions for the seven years he was missing. This is a sad commentary on the way most people spend eight to twelve hours a day. You deserve better.

Information interviewing is, first, a method of career exploration and, second, a way of discovering jobs that are not publicly advertised. It is widely acknowledged as the only way to uncover at least 50 percent of the job market. Essentially, you are going to find out what you could do to earn an income that would best suit you at this time in your career or working life.

A basic premise of this book is that we all live by the choices we make. That is to say, you choose how you spend your time and with whom you go to the movies, for example. It is presumed that by picking up this book, you are in the process of deciding how you will be earning your living next year. Alternatives are what you are looking for. The more research you do, the more geographical locations you are open to, the more career possibilities you explore, the more you will be convinced that you have many more options than you previously thought. Sitting at home mailing out letters won't achieve success. Sitting in your current job wishing someone would rescue you by telling you about a great job just right for you may happen. But it may not. Hundreds of my clients and no doubt tens of thousands of others have successfully dis-

"A man's friends are his magnetisms."
Ralph Waldo Emerson

covered their career direction and have found jobs through the process of research and information interviewing.

By doing this work, you will make new lifelong contacts, learn a lot about yourself, and grow immeasurably through discovering and using your assets and moving ahead despite your perceived or real limitations.

Think of this task as a research project and work on it as though you deserve to be satisfied, want to succeed, and will find work that is a match for your style of intelligence. You want work that demands your strengths, whether creativity, kindness, compassion, dependability, a good education, flexibility, ability to get the job done, salesmanship, communication skills, party planning, typing, pipe fitting, or playing the flute.

If you're truly open to new possibilities, the initial phase of exploration can result in increasing your level of confusion. Since periods of confusion are the only time human beings are forced to think creatively, some confusion is a good thing. Narrowing your options will happen soon enough. Be willing to really mix it up for a while. If it makes you more comfortable, you can set a date to stop researching before you begin so you can be sure that you set the limits and are in control.

As you conduct research in the library and later, in person-to-person conversations, you will naturally define, redefine, and identify exactly what it is you need to know in order to make the necessary decisions about your future. Essentially, you are searching for career possibilities that use your most developed and natural skills, where you will be working at your highest level of competence. Underemployment, i.e., working beneath your abilities, is the cause of most employee dissatisfaction, so look for opportunities that are a bit of a stretch for you.

One of the primary goals of your research project is to build a variety of contacts, either temporary or lifelong. You will find that you already have many kinds of contacts to draw from as you are compiling your list of people to call: those you already know; former co-workers; people you meet during your research, through hobbies, through a spouse, through parents' and volunteer organizations; and names that will be given to you.

After some initial brainstorming, you will prioritize the names by which ones you will contact first. One successful mid-level manager said that the most important turning point of his research campaign was when he "decided to just call shamelessly everyone I could think of." That kind of approach (where you just let go of your ego's chatter about people not wanting to be bothered with you or not having time or some other reason not to make the calls) is the way to go forward.

Obtaining information interviews takes practice. Your telephone skills and your ability to schedule appointments will improve with the number of calls you make. Your confidence will grow and your presentation will become smoother with practice.

Equally important to making those initial contacts is keeping up with them. As a service to companies, I occasionally provide career counseling to "trailing spouses," i.e., the significant others of people who relocate because of job opportunities. The husband in this case got a new job, and the wife was a professional woman who left her job behind. (This is true in 89 percent of relocations involving trailing spouses.) I gave her some help, and she went out to look for a job. Two months later she called me to tell me how it was going. She had not been able to find a job she wanted. I had heard from a networking contact earlier that same day that she needed an employee to do a part-time accounting job. From what I knew of my former client and the businesswoman, it seemed like a good fit. They have been working together long enough now for the job to become full time. After two months of not hearing from a former client, I had not thought of her for the job, but I did after she called me. She got an opportunity because she kept her network active by making calls and letting people know that she was still looking.

In another example, a client who was in a painful employment situation came to me to begin a search for a career change. We went through an exploration process that included interest testing, personality testing, counseling, and self-esteem-building exercises. She conducted information interviews in fields outside her current one to find out what else would interest her. Her decision was that she wanted to leave the current job where she was under-employed and wanted her next position to be similar to one she had five years earlier. So, the next assignment was reactivating the old network that had been neglected because of long hours with the current company. It took a month for her to reach one of those significant contacts: A month of calling and leaving messages back and forth, not getting calls back because he was out of town. She persevered. They did have lunch eventually and in the course of the conversation he offered her her ideal job, with a 10 percent increase in pay! She wouldn't have recognized it as her ideal job if she had not done the self-search process and would not have connected with him had she given up easily

"Where is your Self to be found? Always in the deepest enchantment that you have experienced."
Hugo von Hofmannsthal

in trying to reach him. He was simply busy, not trying to avoid her or thinking that she wasn't important. The moral of these stories is obvious: Stay in touch with the people on your list of contacts.

This project requires an investment of time and energy and a good attitude. Since no one truly owes you the courtesy of their time and information, your approach will determine to some extent the speed at which you are successful. Since your own time management system will be your closest ally, you will want to devise an organizational system that helps you get the most accomplished in the least amount of time. This book will show you how to get organized and build a strategy for your research.

Information interviewing is not job interviewing. It is a network-building, information-gathering phase of a complete and thorough search for a good job. In his book *Moving Up* (J. B. Lippincott Co., 1971) executive recruiter Eli Djeddah emphasized what most job seekers and career changers simply refuse to accept: At least half of the jobs that you could get hired into are positions that are created for the applicant. The applicant who understands this has a much better chance of finding a job that she enjoys and finds satisfying than the applicant who puts herself at the mercy of the newspaper want ads.

My experience in Personnel (Human Resources) is congruent with others'. We have all been called by hiring managers who wanted us to do the required paperwork and a functional interview with someone they had already decided to hire, based on their conversations with the applicant, now known as a New Hire. "How did you find her?" personnel people always ask.

Networking is always the response. The New Hire and the hiring manager met at the club, through their last company, through a friend of someone on the staff; the New Hire found my number somehow and called me out of the blue one day. These hiring managers did not run an ad in the paper—they don't want to talk to that many applicants. They have rarely called an employment agency or a headhunter (they usually aren't authorized to spend the 15 to 25 percent of the position's annual salary—the typical recruitment fee). Often, Personnel didn't even know there was an opening, because there wasn't. The person who secured the job simply came around, talked about himself in a positive way, and the hiring manager realized that he needed him.

Information interviews are useful at several junctures of a career. Sometimes called advice interviews, they are one of the best avenues for learning about what's happening in a variety of fields and industries. Use information interviewing to build and maintain a professional network and to enhance and expand your career awareness.

In a meeting with a successful consultant recently, I asked how she built her business. She replied that all of her previous work experience had been in banking. When the banking industry went through considerable reorganizing, she conducted information interviews and discovered that so much consulting work was available that she did not have to seek out a new job. When you meet new people, ask a question to let them know that you are interested in them. You can learn so much just by asking.

If you are still not convinced that information interviews could help you, put a check next to the following items that you consider valuable.

❏ Build your confidence for job interviews.

❏ Expand your job market information.

❏ Become a more impressive job candidate if you have done some "professional homework."

❏ Discover the titles of your Ideal Jobs so you can build your future toward a goal instead of constantly wanting to move away from dissatisfying experiences.

❏ Find out about career paths you did not know existed.

❏ Discover what the best personality is for the jobs you are considering, so you can match it against yours. Is there a good fit?

❏ Meet new people.

❏ Deepen your understanding of the world of work in a variety of settings.

❏ Have firsthand current information rather than data from printed material researched three to ten years ago that you may find at the library.

Employment Interviews:
1. Employer seeks you out
2. Employer sets up the appointment
3. Employer asks the questions
4. Employer draws the conclusions

Information Interviews:
1. You seek out contacts
2. You set up the appointments
3. You ask the questions
4. You draw the conclusions

"To know oneself, one should asset oneself."
Albert Camus

❏ Learn to mentally connect talking to strangers about jobs as a low stress experience, enhancing your communication skills.

❏ Ask for information so you learn how to be in control of the discussion, an invaluable business skill.

❏ Potential employers have a chance to meet you at your best.

❏ Find out what you should be reading and which professional associations you should join to remain up-to-date in your areas of interest and ability.

❏ Clarify and state your initial goals and redefine them each time you get more information, so you will be walking down the path toward your dream job, carried by the process, instead of being paralyzed by not knowing exactly what you should be doing and being embarrassed by it.

❏ Have an opportunity to experience yourself grow through shyness, low self-esteem, or inhibitions about talking to people.

❏ Unashamedly put your career into your schedule as a number-one priority for a while. The shakes and turns of the job market require that experienced workers make their career goals a top priority at least four times during their lives.

❏ Be a project manager for a project with short- and long-term goals that you have complete control over. It's good management experience, and it's an opportunity to do it your way.

❏ Gain self-knowledge as a by-product of the ideal job exploration process.

❏ Avoid being stuck in a job you hate for twenty years.

❏ Take control of your future—an exhilarating experience.

❏ Clarify the weaknesses in your education, skill base, and personal development. Areas for choice and growth will become apparent to you so you can change or accept them.

❏ Learn to appreciate what is intelligent, skilled, artistic, healing, organized, and talented about you so you can capitalize on it.

❏ Find out what motivates you, and you will find out what you can live without or compromise on.

❏ Work around or get past personnel departments and talk to hiring managers who can give you more contacts at other companies in other industries.

❏ Develop your listening skills.

❏ Improve your social skills.

❏ Renew your belief in the goodness of people and their innate desire to be helpful.

❏ Be proud of yourself for doing something tough, i.e., contacting strangers and asking for their time.

❏ Learn a skill that will serve you well throughout your entire life: the development of your will, i.e., to keep on going even when it is hard, you are embarrassed, and you don't want to.

❏ Establish and expand your professional "network" and make new friends.

❏ Everyone you establish a contact with will also be looking for a job for you if you make a good impression, thank them, communicate openly about your abilities and goals, and stay in contact with them, making your search more efficient.

"Information Interviewing is an important step in the career development process. Once you have identified your skills, interests, values, preferences and researched the occupations to give you a working knowledge of them, this step can help you validate your choices. It is critical that you test your perceptions with individuals doing the work. You may also save valuable time by asking, "What would you do differently if you were starting where I am now???"—Shirley Weishaar, Associate Director, Center for Career Planning, Mills College, Oakland, CA.

How to do Information Interviewing

Learning how to do information interviewing is a skill that will be valuable to you whether you are a recent graduate, a well-seasoned professional, a home executive reentering the work-for-money scene, or are planning to retire. You now see that information interviewing is a method for building a professional network, finding a mentor, searching for the right job, finding out what it takes to have your own business, building contacts for selling yourself, selling a product, and getting the information you need to make a retirement decision.

Conducting research in the library and through information interviewing has been recommended by virtually every book ever written on the subject of job searching, but most books primarily focus on what career you should go into or how to interview and write a resume. None give you detailed direction on how to do the in-person research they so wisely tell you to do; hence, this book.

Information Interviewing: How to Tap Your Hidden Job Market is centered on you—on building your skills. Attention is given to what works. The examples included here are based upon real-life situations taken from a practicing career counselor's experience. Step by step, each chapter teaches you what you need to do to get started and to follow through to success. You will be actively involved in mastering the techniques before you finish reading the book through the first time.

Information Interviewing: How to Tap Your Hidden Job Market gives you more than theory. You will make progress in your networking efforts by using the tips on what to say to start conversations. The contacts you have been avoiding calling will be won over when you use the script we help you write. You will find sample letters for almost any situation you will encounter—just rewrite them to fit the people you are addressing. You'll learn how to explore better job possibilities within your current company, consider your options for a mid-life career change, find out whether you qualify for the jobs you want, and discover your ideal position.

Information interviewing is your key to job and career search satisfaction. Invest in this process before you set foot in a job interview. Your first time, this time, finally—get a real job! You deserve it.

Chapter 2

Where to Begin

Where you should begin depends in part on where you are in the process of life. For example, recent graduates looking for their first professional position will go a slightly different route than an adult who is considering changing careers.

A Generic Sample Path

The following steps are meant as an example of how one person could progress through the process of identifying and defining the problems specific to their situation, working to find solutions, and planning the action to take.

Step 1. Take time for self-assessment

Chapter three contains exercises to help you evaluate what you like, what you want, and how you might best carry it out. Chapter four discusses ways to shore up your self-confidence.

Step 2. Go to the library for half a day

Chapter five gives you an overview of the job market, while chapter six gives you the basics on library research.

In the card catalog look up these topics: career, job, work, resume, self-employment. Take half a dozen books off the shelf and look through them, then take more. You will find that reading about how others have built careers around their interests and skills will give you ideas for job possibilities and people to contact. Most libraries have at least fifteen books on how to write a

resume. The sample resumes are based on actual careers and will show you how one set of skills can take an individual in many different directions. For example, in her book *The Resume Catalog: 200 Damn Good Examples* (published by Ten Speed Press, 1989), Yana Parker outlines two hundred resumes she wrote for her resume service in Berkeley, California.

Step 3. Set up a system of organization for your research project

Most of what you need to get started is provided in chapter seven. Essentially, you need a method of tracking both tasks to be completed as well as your progress to keep you motivated; a system for recording the names, addresses, and numbers of contacts; a notation of calls made, to be made, letters sent, and thank you letters to be sent. The forms I've provided will work, or you can design your own.

Step 4. Conduct practice information interviews with three people

The three practice interviews can be friends and family, co-workers, fellow students, an instructor, a boss, the paper boy, or someone you have wanted to meet. These are for practice and may or may not reveal any fabulous career opportunities for you. In chapter eleven there are sample questions to use until you develop your own list.

Step 5. Build a list of initial contacts

Chapter eight discusses building a network. Your initial contacts will be people you know and have met in the course of your personal, student, and professional life.

Step 6. Send letters and make calls to people on your contact list

Chapters nine and ten describe the process of writing affective letters and making telephone calls to your prospects. Tell them you are conducting a research project on jobs and careers and would like to talk to them about their work.

Step 7. Keep abreast of what's out there

Go back to the library. Look through the want ads in the weekend papers and the Tuesday *Wall Street Journal* to find out what kinds of jobs are most frequently advertised and what kinds of companies are advertising. Since 70 percent of the jobs that people are hired for never appear in ads, this is only one part of your research, not necessarily the way you will find your dream job. Even if most of the ads are placed by companies hiring engineers or accountants, you will want to know for future reference what their products are; you will often find these products described in detail in their recruitment advertisements.

Step 8. Conduct some real information interviews

Review chapter eleven. Write up your lists of questions. Go get 'em!

Step 9. Send thank you letters

Refer to chapter nine for examples of thank you letters. Follow up on the leads you received. Remember that thank you letters can reinforce your good impression, making you stand out in the person's mind.

Step 10. Revisit the library, and check out a career center

This time your library research should focus on jobs you think would interest you and on the companies in your preferred and second-choice geographical areas.

High schools, junior colleges, universities, Jewish Community Centers, and trade schools have career centers. Many large metropolitan areas also have publicly funded community career centers at YWCAs and other locations. Usually you can visit them for a day for no cost or pay $2.00 to use their libraries with information about jobs and companies in the area. Check the Yellow Pages and refer to the back of *What Color Is Your Parachute?*

Step 11. Make telephone calls and send letters to those you would like to meet and interview in the future

Once again, refer to chapters nine and ten for examples and ideas.

"In doing we learn."
George Herbert

Step 12. Make a career decision based on your research and information interviews

Chapter twelve contains decision-making tools to help you pull together all the information you have accumulated about yourself and the career possibilities you want to pursue. When you have completed the steps and have made a decision, you will feel fully prepared to begin the job search, confident that you are headed in the right direction and armed with a network to aid you in reaching your goals.

New Graduates

The new graduates I have counseled are in the enviable position of being open minded about the possibilities in the world of work. If you are a recent graduate you may feel overwhelmed by thinking you have too many possibilities and you don't know where to begin. Work your way through all of the activities in this book, beginning with the self-assessments in chapter three, and follow the guidelines for research, telephone calls, and correspondence in chapters nine and ten. By the time you reach the decision-making materials in chapter twelve, you will be able to make a decision about where to begin your career.

If you are still in school you are at a definite advantage. Conducting the exercises will provide you with the opportunity to set your career in the right direction from the day you graduate. No false starts for you.

The special problems new grads may encounter include little or no work experience to guide them easily into selecting a job, experience only in retail sales or child care, and too little information about the twenty thousand types of jobs that exist.

One of my clients is a good example of someone who did the homework and succeeded. During high school, Tyler had only worked in the construction jobs his dad got for him during the summer. It was the only work he knew, but he was sure he did not want to choose construction as a career. Somehow, it didn't satisfy something in him. His father is an engineering executive, and he felt that it was too much pressure and too much desk work for him. Tyler's hobby was off-road motorcycle racing and riding jet skis. At first he wondered if he could find a way to make athletics into a career. But, knowing some professional motorcycle riders, he couldn't quite imagine himself living the life on the road that is required.

After going through the process of self-assessment, library research, and information interviews, he chose a career that surprised everyone who knew him, including his parents. He decided to become a sports nurse, helping people who experienced sports injuries. Tyler had broken his fair share of bones and had been to chiropractors and physical therapy dozens of times and wanted to help people he could relate to. He went to college for five years, now has an RN, is working in home health care, and is buying a house in a rural area. A dream come true. He still wants to become a specialist in sports medicine, but for now he's getting experience and "paying his dues" by working for an agency that serves home-bound patients. In addition to the experience he's gaining, he is making valuable contacts in sports medicine that will help him reach his long-term career goal.

Remember, when Tyler first came to me he had no idea that nursing would be his choice. He had never considered it. His mother had spoken of wanting to be a nurse when she was young, but that childhood conversation was his only contact with the thought of it as a career. Be prepared with an open mind as you proceed to discover your future. There is no way to predict what path you will take.

High school students and college graduates alike tend to think of themselves as having too few skills. By the time most of us graduate from college we know we have test-taking skills, and showing-up-for-class skills (most of us), and we can write a passable paper. When graduation approaches, getting out of school becomes the major focus, even though we may not have a clue what we're going to do the day after. Many new grads continue with the type of work that they were doing before graduation and quickly become disillusioned with the education system for not preparing them for something better. It does prepare you for something better, and you can find out what that is and pursue it.

When you complete the skills assessment in chapter three, you'll have a list of the skills you can use in the work you pursue, as well as how you want to design your life using them to satisfy your needs and desires.

"Every beginning is hard."
German proverb

Career Changer

While the information in this book applies in general to career and job searching at any age, men and women who are forty and older have considerable life experiences that make their goals and objectives different from those of a new or recent graduate. The life experiences and the changes in life values that occur at mid-life and later make you less confused and naive about the world of work and, at the same time, more particular about your next position.

An overwhelming majority of mid-life career changers are glad that they made a change, whether the final impetus for the move came from themselves or from the company where they worked. A high school teacher I know became a stock broker at forty; a career secretary is now in sales; an advertising executive now owns a winery.

Throughout my clients' experiences, networking is consistently reported as the most effective method of securing a new, satisfying position or career. Often the most disenchanted explain that while they were working hard, others seemed to be talking all the time. This comment made by a client is typical, "I was up in my office making sales to keep the company going, and there he was drinking with the boys. Well, now he's a vice president at another company, and I'm out here at forty-six trying to start a network." In fact, when managers, executives, and supervisors report their experiences, they note that they worked so hard—eighty to ninety hours a week—for the company that they let their networks dissolve, to their later dismay.

Men and women who are fired or laid off are more likely to make career changes that seem radical—from financial management to bicycle repair shop, for example. Individuals who leave their employer by choice are more likely to go on to positions similar to the ones they just left. For career changers in mid-life, avocations can become mid-life or retirement vocations. Often these individuals rediscover an interest that began in their early twenties that has remained an interest, even if they haven't had time to pursue it.

One day I went into a picture-framing store, and the owner who waited on me recognized me as the professional recruiter who had hired her and her husband into a semiconductor company as engineering managers in the 1980s. They decided in mid-life that they wanted their lives to be more than the seventy-hour-a-week grind; they were tired of the cyclical ups and downs and wanted more freedom over their destiny. They enjoyed working hard but felt that corporate politics took too much of their energy. This couple went through a self-assessment process and decided to buy two framing shops, one for each of them to manage. As a mechanical engineer, she enjoyed working with spatial relationships and had been interested in art during college. Her success in corporate life had held her there for twenty years, but she knew it was never too late to start something new and find satisfying work.

If you are ready for a change but don't know how to make it happen, plan to invest six to twelve months in introspection and preparing. The Generic Sample Path is the basic methodology you should follow, but you will also want to assess your financial situation carefully. A career change could potentially mean a reduction in your disposable income. It doesn't have to, but this may be a compromise you will have to make in order to gain more satisfaction and reduce the stress that comes from doing work that no longer suits you.

Networking is time-consuming and usually requires some evenings at professional associations, the library, and meetings with contacts. For these reasons you must set realistic time goals. Consider how much time each week you can carve out for doing the assignments. You will get it all done, it will just take longer than someone who is free full time.

The strongest reason adults give for wanting to change jobs at mid-life is that the work they are doing no longer satisfies them. Boredom, topping out, and simply being tired of relentless pressures are also given as reasons for wanting change. Most career changers eventually admit, if only to themselves, that their most recent position had become unbearable in some way.

Many of the mid-life changes we see are from positions focused on data and things to work that is personally more rewarding. Some choose law, shop ownership, turning an interest into an income-producing business, training, and consulting. They discover a renewed pride in their accomplishments and a sense of personal growth and development in their new occupations. Many find that the escape from boredom, bureaucracy, paperwork, corporate maneuverings, political infighting, and being driven by others' agendas is like discovering a new life. However, those who left their companies "involuntarily" get relief only after going through the standard stages of grief: shock, disbelief, depression, rebuilding, getting back to normal activity levels, and some financial hardship. If you have

"When men are easy in their circumstances, they are naturally enemies to innovations."
Joseph Addison

lost your position or feel that you must leave because of pressures, the sooner you can view the change as a life event rather than a catastrophe, the sooner you will be able to get on to that new life.

Your attitude toward the life events you are experiencing is key to your eventual success. Surveys indicate that people who involuntarily leave their positions are less likely to view the transition as positive, even though this same group is just as likely to find the move financially and personally rewarding. It's possible that those who just stay in a job they don't like for years until their contribution diminishes and they are fired are going to be unhappy no matter where they work. That won't be you.

Guidelines for Mid-Life Career Changers

Step 1. Cultivate acquaintances outside your current company and your current industry

Many adults between jobs find that they finally have time to become involved in their community through the arts, commissions, and other nonprofit organizations. When they make the time, they find that through these affiliations they find support, satisfaction, and rewards. When you leave the contacts at your current company, you also leave the environment where you made decisions, exercised your competitive muscle, and knew the answers. Becoming involved in something outside yourself will provide many of those same rewards, plus rebuild your base of contacts and support. And, job leads often come from unpredictable directions.

If you are currently employed, shop for a new professional association to join by attending meetings of those that hold an interest for you. Most newspapers have listings of their meetings with a contact telephone number, so you can find out more before you commit the time to going. Attend one meeting each month until you find a group that meets your personal and professional needs.

Also, begin to reestablish contact with people you have met at conferences, through classes, and at other companies, scheduling lunch, coffee meetings, or simply calling them regularly to talk about what you each are doing. Put it on your calendar to make calls weekly, for example, on Friday afternoons.

Put your energies into something new. This is probably the essence of networking—to go beyond familiar activities, people, and responsibilities you now enjoy, in order to broaden your circle of acquaintances, expand your thinking into new realms, and learn new skills.

Step 2. Take a class

Go to classes as a way to discover new interests, meet new people, improve your hireability, and prevent bitterness about the unwanted changes in your industry. It is common for career changers in mid-life to pursue graduate degrees, complete four-year degrees, or reeducate themselves for entrepreneurial ventures.

Step 3. Return all phone calls

Everyone who calls you when you are working should be given the courtesy of a return call, not only because they may have a job lead for you in the future, but also because it's common courtesy. The people I have counseled who have the most difficult time getting courtesy interviews, information, leads, and research interviews are the ones who openly admit that they don't return their own calls and certainly don't "waste time" on granting information interviews. No one should be ignored.

Step 4. Get over your awkwardness about asking for help

People may not know what to say to you if you leave your job, but you can set the tone and bridge communication by squaring with yourself and setting a positive, relaxed tone in your interactions with neighbors, former co-workers, and staff. One of the lessons you can learn through this process is that people want to help you— sometimes even the ones who were instrumental in the final events that led to your change in jobs.

Step 5. Look for opportunities to give back to the network

When you talk to an employer and find out about an opening they want to fill, call someone in your network and tell them about it. They may know someone who is looking for that job. When you meet others who are "available during the day," find out what they are look-

"To live is to function. That is all there is in living."
Oliver Wendell Holmes

ing for and connect them with possible contacts. Be aware of others' needs; you'll feel good about the opportunities that will come of it.

Step 6. Get help from a career counselor or career changers' support group

Up to 75 percent of mid-life career and job changers find professional career counseling help to be useful. An entire industry has been built to satisfy the needs of people who want career advice. You can find career counselors who charge by the hour, nonprofit career centers that operate on a sliding-fee scale, and career counseling businesses that sell packaged programs.

All career guidance providers should agree to meet with you briefly before you select the one to use. If you go to one of the companies, rather than to an individual or a nonprofit, ask the person who talks with you who will provide the counseling services you are buying. At a few of these companies the person you talk to first is a trained salesperson—some provide no counseling at all, and a couple of them charge fees in the thousands of dollars. Be sure you meet the counselor who would work with you before you sign any contract. Look for someone with whom you feel confident and personally comfortable. Many very reputable and effective career counselors chose counseling or teaching as their first career and have little work experience themselves. This should not be a barrier to your selection process, but ask some questions regarding the fields from which most of their clients come. If you have an interest in a particular field, find out if they have ever worked with anyone who had an interest in that field. Over the years, I was able to provide many leads for information interviews to my clients.

Career counselors should provide self-report quizzes, values assessment tools, and personality style questionnaires for the self-assessment phase. They must know how to guide you through a research process, or they will point you in a direction with which they are familiar rather than an unusual position that you could uncover through research.

Ask them how they help clients make a career decision and how long, on average, it usually takes their clients to arrive at the end of the counseling. My experience is that it takes an adult an average of three months to go through the initial phases, then an additional three to six months to show significant movement toward the goals they established.

If you also need help composing a resume and conducting a job search, ask to see resumes they have prepared for previous clients and what they usually include in the way of job search help.

They should not balk at answering these kinds of inquiries and should have ready answers if they have experience. If you are satisfied with their answers and rapport has been established through this initial conversation, you have identified a good place to begin.

The cost of career counseling varies widely. Hourly fees range from $50 to $125, depending on the education and experience of the provider. If you contract for a series of testing, counseling, resume-writing, and job-search support expect to pay from $1500 to $7,000. Buyer beware. Do not agree to pay in full in advance for a package program. Agree to pay for the first phase and see how it goes between you and the company and the counselors.

Finding a good career counselor is like finding a good dentist, doctor, or marriage counselor. Ask your friends if they have heard of anyone they could recommend and contact your church or synagogue for referrals that they may know of. You can look in the back of *What Color Is Your Parachute?* (R.N. Bolles) for counselors in your area. As a last resort look in the yellow pages and call a few to find out how they operate their practice.

Step 7. Establish a new routine

If you are unemployed, build a new routine around a workday schedule, including exercise, dressing, and planning your day and week. Exercise is an acknowledged antidote to depression, as are improved diet, reduced alcohol consumption, increased time with loved ones, and scheduled time for the rediscovery of a hobby.

Step 8. Think about moving

Consider relocating to a more rural area, to a different climate, or to a less expensive area where the quality of the school system is less of a consideration now. Com-

"Our friends show us what we can do, our enemies teach us what we must do."
Goethe

"Work keeps at bay three great evils: boredom, vice, and need."
Voltaire

peting for money and status is clearly a significant ingredient in the values of youth, but is somewhat less important to mid-life adults. Go to the places you are considering and conduct in-depth research on the area while you are adjusting to your new phase of life. When you get back you will have had an important period of renewal and be ready to tackle the next step.

Step 9. Deal with your personal issues

Most of you must begin an earnest search for your next position as soon as you possibly can, because it's better for your career and better for your mental health. The personal issues confronting you may include self-esteem, marital satisfaction, family issues, finances, and the like. While you have been working eighty hours a week, much of your personal life may have been on the back burner. In the time between jobs, it can all come home to roost. You may find that you will blow the first few interviews you arrange because your self-confidence is flagging, you are becoming reacquainted with your family, or you are preoccupied with financial concerns. While these issues never get completely resolved for anyone, an investment of time focusing on them now could put you on surer footing for the tasks ahead.

Step 10. Develop a portfolio of your achievements

You can approach this in several ways. One way is to write an annotated autobiographical outline of your life that includes where you were, what you were doing, what you liked and didn't like about it, and what made you leave that activity. Another way is to write down the major accomplishments of your life by life phase; in five-year segments; or in "free style," a few hundred pages about the events, decisions, outcomes, trials and successes of your life.

If that task seems too enormous to begin, start with this week. Jot down on your calendar or in a notebook what you accomplish week by week, and build a file of them. Then think about previous jobs, committees, organizations, academic years, and hobbies and make notes about where you've been, what you contributed, and what you found satisfying.

Step 11. Define your dream job

As a way to help you clarify your goals for the future, write a help wanted ad or a description of your perfect job. Information interviews, library research, conversations with people in a variety of career fields, and increased self-knowledge will create changes in what your dream job is from month to month, so let it evolve. Just as your life experiences have changed the way you see yourself and your future, so will the process of searching for what would be ideal for you. Plan to reformulate and redefine the description to reflect what you are learning.

Step 12. Get feedback from previous colleagues, co-workers, and friends

Use the Personal/Profession Career Survey to get feedback from people who know your strengths and-skills and who may have an opinion about what you could do next as a career. Make as many copies of the form as you think you would find useful. My suggestion is that you ask a minimum of six people and no more than twenty. When all of the forms are returned to you, tally the responses by category and look for common themes. If you received confusing feedback from someone, ask them to clarify what they wrote. If a common career direction weaves throughout all of the forms and it is something you have not considered, go ahead and do some research.

A surprising number of the adults I have counseled have told me what they wanted to do without hearing themselves say it. They had been talking about it and hoping for it for so many years that they had lost touch with the desire as a real possibility. Finally at mid-life they can take action and do what they could only talk about before. Sometimes our thoughts have to be reflected back to us. You may have listened to a person you know talk about being happiest when organizing large events, teaching, preparing food for hundreds of people at fund-raisers, or being involved in the start-up of a small organization. People who have been listening to you talk about your "someday" dream may have really been listening. Find out from them what they think would be a good move for you now.

"You eat, in dreams, the custard of the day."
Alexander Pope

Personal Professional Career Survey For _____

Date _____

Dear _____,

By completing this information, you will help in an assessment process that is very important to the future plans of the individual whose name appears on the top line. Please provide your considered opinion in response to the items below. Use extra paper if necessary.

1. How long have you known the person?

2. Please indicate your relationship: co-worker, friend, spouse, relative, other.

3. What do you consider to be his/her primary interests?

4. What abilities do you most admire in him/her?

5. What accomplishments does s/he seem to be proudest of?

6. Which of his/her skills would you like to see developed better?

7. What job or career would be a good one for this person?

8. Please describe his/her characteristics in the following areas:

    * Intellectual (thinking, analyzing, studying, problem-solving)

    * Artistic (unstructured, creative, imaginative)

    * Social (sensitive, enjoys interactions and conversation, helper)

    * Physical (solves practical problems by fixing things, active)

    * Entrepreneurial (salesperson, leader, likes to be in charge)

    * Detail-oriented (responsible, task-oriented, well-organized)

Thank you for your opinions.

Please return this form to the person whose name appears at the top right corner.

Company Man or Woman

If you now work in a midsize or relatively large company, it is possible that your dream job is just a department, cubicle, or building away. Information interviewing and networking are the perfect method to use to find out.

The advantage to staying with the same company is that your "service" is continuous, i.e., your benefits, pension plan, salary progression, and perks continue. It has been noted that sometimes the people who are promoted are those who stay with the company through thick and thin. That is not to say that these employees just sat around and waited, but industry observers have noted that if one stays long enough to build an impressive record of service, promotions will come. There is a lot to be said for commitment and loyalty.

For example, one of my clients is now a director at the company where he stuck it out during an industry downturn. The company hit hard times, and many of the brightest found other jobs at the first sign of trouble. By the time the company turned around two years later, he was literally the only employee remaining in his department. Through the layoffs and reorganizations, he did the work that had to be done, even though the low morale made it very difficult some weeks. When the company hired back the same number of people they had laid off, he was the obvious choice to head the department.

Another common denominator among professionals who have a solid, distinctive work history is a breadth of experience that applies to the company's needs. You can choose to get that experience in your current company if it allows "lateral transfers" and has learning opportunities available. Until you become informed, you really can't decide whether your employer has what you need in order to allow you to accomplish your goals. First, you have to figure out your goals.

Well-networked people have better opportunities to make the moves necessary to get ahead because they hear about the openings first and have made contact with professionals within the company who are willing to sponsor them.

The two main ingredients to networking within your company are commitment and commitment. It will take time, effort, planning, and follow-through to make it happen.

Guidelines for Getting a Better Job in Your Company

Step 1. Talk with your supervisor

That is, if it is possible. Even if you report to someone whom you would guess is not on your side in this matter, you may be surprised to find out that she or he is willing to help. Your conversation should be private, so you will make an appointment to talk when they can give you their full attention. (Monday mornings are usually not a good time. Five minutes after the person walks in is definitely not a good time.) Tell them that you are planning your career and would like to look around the company for positions that would interest you in the future.

Many corporate hierarchies are set up to reward managers based on the size of their staffs. Managers who do not think they are secure in their status for other reasons will engage in what is called "empire-building," which means that if you leave and they do not have permission to replace you, they will have lost some of their status (called "losing headcount"). In addition, recruiting, interviewing, training, and getting used to new people costs time and money. For these reasons, your immediate supervisor may not be encouraging and supportive. Plus, you are probably doing a good job for him or her and replacing your talents would be a big job.

In all honesty, it may take you six months to a year to locate your ideal job, so you can reassure your supervisor that you are planning for the future and this does not mean that you are ready to leave. She or he may ask you what you see yourself moving toward and may be able to modify your responsibilities in order to help you meet your growth needs.

Step 2. Start your self-search

You must look within yourself and ask the questions: What have I done in school, career, hobbies, and community work that was productive and satisfying? What was dissatisfying? Organizational psychology says that satisfiers are usually in the realm of money and status, and dissatisfiers are usually in the realms of appreciation, intellectual challenge, comfort with peers, and how their family and friends regard their careers. What have you done that you liked? If you have been working for ten years or more and the answer is nothing, you could probably benefit considerably from library research on the whole gamut of available jobs. Consider career interest and ability testing as a way to open more avenues of choice.

Case Example: Let's say that you have an interest in efficiency and enjoy working with information. Your garage and kitchen cabinets are organized, your checkbook is usually balanced, and your reports are turned in on time. You prefer not to work in customer service and sales jobs because the frequent contact with people you do not know is exhausting for you. What jobs in your company require an organized, detail-oriented person, but no public contact? We could guess: accounting, purchasing, order entry, manufacturing, corporate benefits, production control, and admissions and records (in an academic or health care environment).

Step 3. Evaluate your past and current jobs

List the parts of your current and previous jobs that you have liked, put up with, and disliked. Then research jobs in general (see the chapter on library research) and the tasks which are part of positions in typical companies. Betsy Collard's *The High Tech Career Book* (published by Crisp Publications, 1988) is an excellent reference, even if you aren't in or interested in high tech, because there are thorough descriptions of jobs and how they fit into a typical company's organization chart.

Step 4. Go through the information interview process

Start with completing five Information Interviews with family and friends. Include your boss or one of his or her peers, if you can.

The culture of your company may or may not support employees exploring career change on their own. Some want people to stay where they are for a variety of reasons, most of which come down to not liking change or being afraid that you would tell your previous supervisor about mistakes made in the new department. Ask co-

"Work is half one's life—and the other half, too."
Erich Kastner

workers if they know anyone who has changed careers within the organization, and ask someone in the human resources department what the company policy is. Know that the human resources representative may be obligated to tell your boss that you asked the question. Think all of this through beforehand and do it in a way that doesn't limit your success with your current boss should you decide to say where you are.

Step 5. Explore the terrain

When you have a sense of what you do well and what you like, you are ready to explore the terrain. In the previous example, the individual would ask his or her peers if they know anyone in purchasing, accounting, or admissions. If so, that would be the first networking name; if they don't, see the company newsletter or annual report, or ask the operator to get the names of potential contacts.

Step 6. Write your telephone script and one-minute introductions

See chapter ten for instructions on telephone scripts and your one-minute introduction. Be prepared for any questions, then set up appointments. You want to talk with them for twenty or thirty minutes as part of researching ways to use your skills within the company other than in your current position. Assure the person that you are not looking for a job in their group or department at this time, but that you need some information and want to improve your understanding of what the other groups do and how the big picture fits together.

What's different about your information interviews is that you are a known entity is this organization. When you conduct these meetings you will no doubt be asked who you know in the department and why you want to change careers. Prepare answers to these questions that reflect well on your previous and current supervisors, point out what you have learned through your experience, and tell why you are considering this particular work as a career move.

Step 7. Get organized

In every other way, your process will be like the one described throughout this book. You will have to set up a system of organization, develop call sheets, and track your progress in order to maintain momentum. It's not easy to carve out time from your current responsibilities, but you will benefit from the effort.

"Good order is the foundation of all good things."
Edmund Burke

Chapter 3

Self-Assessment

The path toward finding the right career begins with a very important premise: You have a choice. Once you understand the full implications of this simple statement the more empowered you become. You are no longer at the mercy of background, circumstance, or the local economy, because you have a choice. There is a wide gap, however, between knowing that you have a choice and actually knowing how to make a decision.

Regardless of where you are in your career, it is helpful to take a little time to assess, or reassess, your thoughts, feelings, attitudes, hopes, and dreams. The following exercises are designed to help you in this process.

Professional and Personal Self-Assessment

A lot has been said about the fact that how you perceive yourself and your experiences influences your world view and hence the choices you make. If you distributed the feedback form in chapter two to at least six people, you know how others see your talents and interests. This chapter will help you take stock of your past experiences and your present goals and attitudes toward work. The information that you will gain about yourself by thoughtfully completing these questionnaires can illuminate the path ahead.

Thought-Provoking Questionaire

What do you like to do?

Where do you want to live?

What are you doing when you lose track of time?

How much money do you need?

Waht do people compliment you on?

What do you want to do and accomplish before you die?

Should you take skill, ability, and interest tests?

What are your goals for one, three, five, and ten years from now?

Describe what your life was like and what you were doing at a time when you respected yourself the most.

"If the vision we have of ourselves comes from the social mirror— from the opinions, perceptions, and paradigms of the people around us—our view of ourselves is like a reflection in the crazy mirror at the carnival."
Stephen Covey, Principle Centered Leadership

Values

Values form the foundation of your personal mission and the behaviors you use to attain your goals. For example, what quality of work do you think is a job well done? Does a task have to be completed perfectly in order to be up to your standards, or are you satisfied with a quick fix? Most of us could name situations in which a quick job is enough, but for some people excellence is the only standard. What about the quantity of work or the speed at which you complete a project? Do you always feel like you could have done more on any given day, or are you content with what you accomplished? These differences among values affect the quality of our relationships with our co-workers, supervisors, and ourselves to the extent that they impact our self-evaluation.

Understanding your values will lead to better decisions about what kind of a work environment you want to find. Are you one of those people who is dissatisfied with your job even though you enjoy the work? Through this values exercise you may discover that your co-workers or managers have divergent values and you just need to make a change to new people, while doing the same type of work.

A common example that I often see in the companies where I consult, is the woman or man who highly values time with family and friends, but works for or with individuals who believe that the job isn't getting done unless everyone works 10 hours a day, six days a week, leaving no leisure time available. In these unhappy situations, the family oriented employee has a harder time gaining respect for the work that they accomplish, even if that work is satisfactory or exemplary. This person needs to find a situation where their forty-hours of work is valued, preferably working with others who have close family and leisure interests.

The Values Assessment activity has three parts: Part 1, rank your values according to their importance to you; Part 2, evaluate how you would respond if access to your most important values were reduced; and Part 3, evaluate how you would respond if access to your most important values were increased.

Values Assessment Activity

Instructions: Read each of the values listed below and think about their relative importance to you. Rank each of the values, using 5 to indicate a value that is most important to you personally, 4 to indicate that it is important most of the time, 3 to indicate that you sometimes value it, 2 to indicate that it's not very important, and 1 to indicate that it is not important for you at all.

Part 1

Personal Values	Rank
Achievement and a sense of accomplishment	
Advancement and career promotion opportunities	
Adventure, excitement, new experiences	
Affection, caring, and being cared about	
Competition, taking risks for winning	
Cooperation, teamwork, community	
Creativity, innovation, experimentation	
Economic security, steady income	
Fame, being recognized as a star or leader	
Freedom, independence to define and pursue my vision	
Friendship, time to be with others	
Health and emotional well-being	
Help others, improve society, be of service	
Inner peace, being at harmony with self	
Integrity, honesty, standing up for beliefs	
Involvement, belonging, participating	
Loyalty, respectfulness, duty	
Order, conformity, tranquillity, please others	
Personal self-fulfillment, use potentials	
Pleasure, leisure, recreation, fun	
Power, influence, control	
Recognition, respect from others	
Religion, closeness to God, beliefs	
Responsibility, accountability	
Self-respect, sense of personal identity	
Wealth, getting rich, having lots of money	
Wisdom, discovering knowledge	

"Being entirely honest with oneself is a good exercise."
Sigmund Freud

Write your top five values on the lines below

Top Five Values	Part 2	Part 3
1.		
2.		
3.		
4.		
5.		

Part 2

Imagine that your next job greatly reduced your ability to have those top five values in your life. Use the following ranking system to indicate your reaction and put the number in the chart above.

> 1 = It wouldn't bother me
> 2 = It would bother me somewhat
> 3 = It would be OK
> 4 = It would bother me a lot
> 5 = It would ruin my life satisfaction

Part 3

Imagine that your next job greatly increased your ability to have those top five values in your life. Use the following ranking system to indicate your reaction and put the number in the chart above.

> 1 = It wouldn't matter
> 2 = It would matter somewhat
> 3 = It would make me happy
> 4 = It would be great
> 5 = It would be a dream come true

Use the information on the chart to identify three values that you consider essential in order for the career you choose to make you happy.

Let's say that your top five values are self-respect, wisdom, achievement, creativity, and advancement. You are considering becoming a research assistant at an oil refinery, a technician, or a gemologist. All three of those possibilities match up with your values, but research assistant would probably be the best fit for your values of wisdom and creativity.

Another way I have used the values assessment to help clients is to carefully review their five least preferred values and think about how many of them are represented in their current working situation. Usually the five least preferred values are highly characteristic of their current work.

Family Career Scripts

What do you say to yourself in response to these directives? You should be a doctor. You should go to college and get another degree. Work shouldn't be so important to you. You have to keep the job you have because you never know when you'll get another one. Your reaction to this kind of directive is based on a set of rules you have for what is suitable, right, and appropriate. For most people, those rules were provided by parents, siblings, teachers, and employers. We live by other people's rules unless we consciously decide to do otherwise.

This self-assessment activity will give you a picture of your family's skills and working history. It is the most popular career insight activity I have ever designed. When it is complete you will understand some of the rules you have about work. A client who is an attorney found that his career choice passed the scrutiny of the Values Assessment, but he still felt that there was something wrong. By completing the Family Career Script he discovered that everyone in his family who was respected was a teacher. Not everyone in the family was a teacher, only those who were spoken of with admiration. He was in a perfectly suitable career for his skills and values and was able to come to terms with his family's rules about the only real career being teaching.

By the way, the reason we use the terms, "Data, People, Things" is because the Federal Government uses those categories in its *Dictionary of Occupational Titles* and *The Occupational Outlook Handbook,* which you'll use at the library when you use chapter six to do career research.

Instructions: Complete the family tree to the best of your knowledge and call family members to find the information you need to fill in the places you are unsure of or do not know about. If Grandpa worked in a factory to support the family and read books in all his free time, put "factory worker" and read fiction on the appropriate line. If Mom stayed at home to care for the family and sewed quilts as a hobby, put both of those on her line. Fill in the career or jobs for your brothers and sisters in the Siblings column, friends and spouses in the appropriate places.

In the section in the middle, write at the top the very first job you ever held: babysitting, paper route, etc. and move down through time writing down all of your jobs. When your form is completed, look at it for patterns. Use the checklist on the following page to help make sense of your Family Career Script.

> "Some are born great, some achieve greatness, and some have greatness thrust upon them."
> *Twelfth Night* Shakespeare

Family Career Script

Grandmother & Grandfather

Father's jobs, skills, special talents

Aunts and Uncles

Grandmother & Grandfather

Mother's jobs, skills, special talents

Aunts and Uncles

Friends' jobs/talents

Significant others

Siblings careers

My job history

Type of work

First job: Age
Next job:
Continue

Children's jobs/skills

DOC:Family Career Script

Checklist for Family Career Script

Instructions: Put the person's name in the left column, and put a check mark in the column that best represents the skills they used most in work or hobby activities. A mechanical technician with a bachelor's degree in engineering technology wondered if he should pursue a different career. His family members' occupations were as follows: His mother was a housewife who enjoyed gardening, all his aunts on that side of the family were housewives who gardened, and his grandfather was a farmer. Working with plants is working with "things," working with farm equipment is "things," so an X is placed in the "things" column for those people. On his father's side of the family, the grandfather and father were both machinists, an uncle is a machinist, and another uncle is an auto mechanic. His brother repairs sewing machines; his sister is a butcher. They all work with "things." His two best friends are both technicians; they work with "things." All of these individuals would have an X in the "things" column. His entire script is for working with "things," and there is no one around him who works serving people in the health or education fields or is a cashier or bookkeeper working with data and information. All of his previous jobs were working with things, also.

Complete your Checklist and look for the patterns.

What patterns did you observe? Do most of the people on your family tree work with data, people, or things?

"After a certain age, the more one becomes oneself, the more obvious one's family traits become."
Marcel Proust

Name of person	Data Information	People Relationships	Things Objects

How about you? What kind of work do you prefer: data, people, or things?

DATA, PEOPLE, THINGS CHECKLIST

Instructions: Place a check mark next to the things you enjoy doing.

DATA	PEOPLE	THINGS
____ edit and write	____ waitress	____ handle equipment
____ balance the checkbook	____ talk on the phone	____ work on cars or bikes
____ read non-fiction	____ volunteer at a hospital	
____ collect stamps		
____ find information		____ chair a committee
____ arrange the chairs		
____ computer operator	____ sales clerk	____ custodian
____ accounting	____ listen to others	____ cooking and housework
____ bookkeeping	____ serve people	____ operate machinery
____ read blueprints	____ persuade	____ coordinate activity
____ summarize data	____ supervise	____ build
____ sell software	____ sell insurance	____ sell in a hardware store
____ find the best price and quality	____ interview to get information	____ repair plumbing and electrical problems
____ analyze information	____ teach	____ control a process
____ coordinate	____ minister	____ do precise operations
____ innovate ideas	____ manage	____ coordinate all processes
____ synthesize ideas	____ coach or mentor	____ set up the work for others
____ Total	____ Total	____ Total

Wheel of Fortune

For people who are visual or creative, making a Wheel of Fortune or Treasure map is an effective method for defining their values and goals. In this activity, you will make a collage of pictures from magazines, words and phrases from the newspaper or magazines, and photographs on a large piece of paper or poster board. Artistic talent is not required. The Wheel of Fortune is helpful because most people react at an emotional level to pictures and words in a way that is similar to the emotional reactions they have to their life circumstances. When your collage is complete you should put it up on the wall in a place where you can see it regularly during your career search. It will serve as a quick reminder of how you want your life to be when you are in your ideal job.

Buy a piece of poster board or butcher paper large enough that you have a surface of at least two feet square, and divide it into sections. Use circles, squares, or colors to separate the sections. Title each section with one of your values or a goal. Your sections could have titles such as: Financial, Co-workers, Creativity, Security, Excitement, Interpersonal relations, Teamwork, Spiritual life, Confidence, Learn new things, Mental clarity, or Career advancement. Look through publications and cut out words and pictures that represent how you want your life to feel, what kinds of people with whom you want to work, how the ideal environment would look. Attach the words and pictures to the paper with glue or tape. Do not limit yourself by depicting what you think you can get; go for the gold and use pictures that are colorful and pleasing. Use crayons or pens to add words, and draw a picture if you can't find one that represents the circumstances that you most want. You can use one picture or several for each section, but don't crowd it so much that you can't see it all easily at a glance.

The process of making a Wheel of Fortune will help you clarify exactly what it is you want most. As you select pictures, you are rejecting others and sorting out your thoughts and feelings about your desires.

Spend time quietly and privately concentrating on your completed project. Consider what the qualities of life you depicted mean to you. How will you feel when you are living that life? Enjoy the daydreaming that results from looking at it.

"The self ... is another one of the discoveries made in the state of nature, perhaps the most important because it reveals what we really are. We are selves, and everything we do is to satisfy or fulfill our selves."
Closing of the American Mind, Allan Bloom

Work Preference

Instructions: Prioritize the 6 groups of descriptive words below. Place a 1 on the line next to the group of words that is most like your work preferences. Place a 6 on the line next to the group of words that is least like your work preferences. Decide where the other four fit between your #1 and your #6, and place the appropriate number on the line.

Priority #

_____ physical, mechanical, practical, concrete, crafts, technical, quiet, action oriented, like structure, outdoors, adventure

_____ investigator, science, ideas, achievement, medical, analysis, introspection, education, task completion, information, theory

_____ flexible, nonconformist, intuitive, self-expression, art and music, involvement, variety, new and unusual, drama, creativity

_____ friends and community, help others, gather people together, interpersonal, achiever, leader, feelings, counselor, outgoing

_____ confident, persuasive, organizer, sales, high energy, manage, drive, endurance, initiator, status, goals, work through people

_____ systematic, routine, detail, efficient, orderly banking, sociable, practical problem solver, clear, quality conscious, follow the rules, facts and data

Interpretation: The groups of words provide a way to think about your preferences, not only as they relate to the work you will perform, but also to the work environments and the people with whom you prefer to associate. You may enjoy working with words and ideas, but do you want to do that in a publishing house, a book store, an advertising agency, or a corporate technical training department? For example, if your #1 choice is friends and community, your number 2 choice is art and music, and your number 3 choice is confident and persuasive, the places you will be happiest and most fulfilled will complement who you are. You probably would not succeed in a work environment where conformity and isolation are enforced.

Personal Style

Instructions: There are four sections of paired words below. You must choose between the pairs of words. Place a check mark next to the words that best describe you at this time.

"Trust thyself; every heart vibrates to that iron string."
Emerson

1. People OR	**2. Fewer People**
___Variety and action	___Focus and concentration
___Fast	___Careful
___People, groups, communication	___Alone, quiet
___Communicate	___Hesitate
___**Total**	___**Total**

3. Ideas OR	**4. Sensitivity**
___Like analysis and logic	___Enjoy pleasing people
___Strive for fairness	___Need praise
___Respond to thoughts	___Values, ethics, integrity
___Firm minded	___Sympathetic
___**Total**	___**Total**

5. Efficiency OR	**6. Blue Sky**
___Prefer standard solutions	___Like new problems
___Established methods	___Dislike repetition
___Precise about facts	___Follow inspirations
___Impatient with complication	___Enjoy complications as puzzles to solve
___**Total**	___**Total**

7. Organized OR	**8. Unstructured**
___Plan the work	___Adapt to change
___Quick decisions	___More careful decisions
___Dislike interruptions	___Starts too many things
___Get it done	___Procrastinate
___**Total**	___**Total**

Scoring: Total the number of marks you have in each of the eight categories. Through these totals you will be able to get a picture of your personal style. Write on the lines below the four categories with the most points.

My four preferences are

1 or 2 _____   3 or 4 _____
5 or 6 _____   7 or 8 _____

Degree of Risk Preference

Instructions: For each of the paired statements below, select the one that is most characteristic of your risk preference in your ideal work situation. Place a check mark by the statement you prefer.

	A	**B**
1.	___Mostly on my own	___Help is always nearby
2.	___Make decisions alone	___Others make most decisions
3.	___General guidelines provided	___Detailed instructions provided
4.	___Often pressed to the limit	___My current skills get the job done
5.	___I am the final authority	___Someone will catch my mistakes
6.	___I can be highly successful or fail	___Never completely succeed or fail
7.	___Constant changes in the job	___Very few changes in the job
8.	___Exciting, but may not last a long time	___Less exciting and more stable

___**Total Column A**   ___**Total Column B**

Scoring: Total the number of check marks in each column. If your Column A total is 5 to 8 you enjoy more risk in your career than most people. If your Column B total is 5 to 8 you probably want minimal risk in your next position. If your totals are somewhat mid-range or equal, go back and change any that you felt could go either way. Try to get a picture of what would be best for you.

Certain employers and professions require one or the other preference. For instance, sales and police work require a tolerance for frequent change, high pressure, and an ability to work without supervision, a high risk profile. People who prefer a calmer, more stable work environment, with detailed rules and supervision, will look for engineering or accounting. Start-up ventures are for risk takers; government and large corporations are for lower-risk tolerance.

Summarize What You've Learned about Yourself

My approach to life is_____

_____

_____

_____

My values are_____

_____

_____

_____

My Family Career Script shows that_____

_____

_____

_____

_____

I most want to work with data, people, or things_____

_____

What I discovered by making a Wheel of Fortune is

_____

_____

_____

_____

My work preferences are for_____

_____

_____

My personal style is_____

_____

My degree of risk preference is_____

_____

_____

"Stability within ourselves"
Bernard M. Baruch

Chapter 4

Self-Confidence/Self-Esteem

Nathanial Branden in *The Six Pillars of Self Esteem* (published by Bantam, 1994) points out that there are two dangers regarding self-esteem. One of them is determinism or fatalism which makes people think that their destiny is set and not much can be done about it. The result of fatalism is passivity and an obstruction of your vision of what is possible. Branden says, "My experience is that most people underestimate their power to change and grow. They believe implicitly that yesterday's pattern must be tomorrow's. They do not see choices that—objectively—do exist.They rarely appreciate how much they can do on their own behalf if genuine growth and higher self-esteem are their goals, and if they are willing to take responsibility for their own lives. The belief that they are powerless becomes a self-fulfilling prophecy."

Usually when your self-confidence is flagging, you feel like doing nothing. It's OK to do nothing about your career search for the length of time it takes to call a friend or go for a walk, but then make yourself do something. List your assets, look through a career book and identify your employable skills, dig in the garden, wash the car. You will find that taking action will almost always cure a period of depression and may be just the breathing space your mind needed to give you a perfect idea.

Executives, artists, scientists, political figures, and writers all escape to beautiful, peaceful, or stimulating surroundings to refresh their creative flow and to problem-solve. These are time-limited and somewhat structured experiences, during which they talk with others who have similar concerns. You can take a scheduled break of two hours, two days, or two weeks, but have goals and intentions for that time. If the goal is to relax and get your mind off the pressures you are experiencing, then do it completely, so that when you return you will be ready to move full steam ahead. If the goal is to walk with a fellow career searcher, talk about what is working and not working for you both. Exchange names and company information, rehearse your 3-minute script, and conduct information interviews with each other.

Branden's definition of self-esteem includes confidence in one's abilities to think and to cope with life's challenges; and, confidence in one's worthiness, deserving to be happy, and enjoy the fruits of one's efforts. Self-esteem is a form of self-confidence. It requires that others treat you with respect and implies that you have the ability to persist at moving toward your valued goals. Flexibility in the face of change, correcting your mistakes, and being cooperative are also part of healthy self-esteem. These are qualities we associate with confident people.

Some people are confused about self-confidence. They believe that the signs of low self-esteem, such as bragging, a loud voice, poor listening habits, and inflexibility are indications of healthy self-esteem. They are quite the opposite. An urgent need to prove one's superiority or inferiority come from the same place: low self-esteem. The set of behaviors usually associated with compliance, low expectations, and the expectation of rejection may be an easier manifestation of poor self-confidence for us to deal with, but a stubborn, moody, intractable, and prejudiced person who insists on being right all the time suffers from the same ailment.

The hallmarks of a healthy self-confidence include a generosity toward others, an ability to form nourishing relationships with others, and an easy acceptance of good outcomes as a result of your own efforts or the helpfulness of people you meet.

Further, Branden says, organizations need people with self-confidence. Workers need to be able to learn new skills, interact with customers and partners from other cultures, be independent, exhibit initiative, and be self-reliant. Building and maintaining healthy self-confidence is a building block of employability. It gives you a sense of control over the events of your life by making you resilient and able to go with the ebbs and flow of the job market. Healthy self-esteem opens the door for you to feel emotionally high and proud of your achievements.

Self-esteem is the result of the conversations you have with yourself. (I know, "What conversations?") Your mood can be greatly influenced by meeting that rude or non-listening, or non-nourishing, person mentioned above, but your self-confidence should not be permanently damaged unless you primarily associate with people who make themselves feel better at your expense.

"Every new adjustment is a crisis in self-esteem."
Eric Hoffer

"In the beginner's mind there are many possibilities, in the expert's mind there are few."
Suzuki

Persistence in the face of frustration is the internal personal quality that often separates success from failure. In the book *Greatness: Who Makes History and Why,* by Dean Keith Simonton (Guilford Press, 1994), the author describes the reason "the rich get richer and the poor get poorer." Suppose that 100 people with equal qualifications are striving for the same goal. Due to the inherent numbers game of the application process, ten of them achieve the goal and are hired, and the other ninety are rejected. There were ten job openings and 100 applicants; the rejections were impersonal. The ten who were hired naturally feel reinforced by being selected. They won the prize and are buoyant. The unlucky ones who were not hired are discouraged by the rejection, and some drop out of any future competition. (We've all heard of, if not met, the waitress with a Ph.D. and the cab driver with books of unpublished short stories.) The process is repeated over the years, with the original ten having a head start. Along the way, more and more of the 100 become discouraged by the competition for the interesting jobs and settle for positions that do not use their talents. Those who hold the course and work around the obstacles put in their path begin to gain recognition as leaders in their field, gain more encouragement, and take on bigger goals. A few more of the original 100 become discouraged by the competition and fall back. In ten years time there are a handful of "stars" remaining in the field. Were they the best of the lot? No, the example states that they were all equally prepared. The original ten were lucky at the beginning. Out of the ninety, the ones who could eventually become one of the "stars" were the ones who persisted in the face of competition and rejection.

Sociologists call the phenomenon I just described the "Matthew effect," named for the Biblical passage from Matthew 25:29: "For to every one who has will more be given, and he will have abundance; but from him who has not, even what he has will be taken away." Simonton goes on to say, "Significantly, mathematical models based on the doctrine of cumulative advantage correctly predict how elitist the population of successful (scientists) will eventually become."

You will need persistence and will power to conduct library research, make twenty phone calls, and meet new people. And, if you persist, you will be surprised at how big the payoff will be. If it isn't easy at the beginning, remember the ninety and don't let early discouragement lead to a decision to give up.

The rest of this chapter is a series of the best suggestions I know for how you can shore up your confidence during this project. Refer to the suggestions in this chapter regularly in the weeks and months ahead. Use one idea a week, and go back to your favorites. If, after using the ideas in this chapter, you want more activities, I recommend a workbook by Connie Palladino, *Developing Self-Esteem: A Positive Guide for Personal Success* (Crisp Publications, 1989). Dr. Palladino says in the introduction, "Self-esteem is a personal trait that can be improved by any person willing to commit his or her self to the task of positive self development."

Exercises To Build, Shore-up, and Maintain Your Confidence Level

The most common reasons that people feel bad is that they are criticizing themselves or other people and resisting the events in their lives. In science we learn that resistance is more powerful and uses more energy than creating. It's the same with human thought. The fastest route to feeling confident and eager to face life is to plan to feel good. The suggestions you'll read here work. If building self-esteem is new to you, choose one method and try it out; progress will come. Watch for positive changes in your attitude and your ability to bounce back. You may also notice improvements in your physical stamina.

Calling Cards

One of the actions you can take to boost your self-confidence when meeting new people is to have calling cards printed. They are a quality investment at a cost of under $20 for 500. When you're at a party, a networking meeting, or an Information Interview and someone asks for your card so they can have a handy reference for your telephone number, you'll feel more confident if you have cards in your purse, pocket, or wallet. Have them printed to look like the card of someone at your professional level. Printers often have good advice on what is standard business form. A word of caution: When the cards have been typeset, you have to approve the proof before the cards are yours. It is best either to take the proof away from the printer's office overnight or take someone with you to check it with you. Otherwise, you'll have 500 cards with errors, and

"The best way to find current information is to talk to people already working in the career field that interests you. Offer to meet for breakfast, lunch or coffee. You are asking for a person's time. These informational experiences are considered part of the job search. Know what the questions are that you will have to ask in order to get the information that you need."— Joan Belshin, Career Counselor, Director, Career Guidance, Life's Decisions, Sacramento, CA.

believe me, I have tried to think of ways to use up old business cards to no avail.

Calling card format before you know your career goal:

> Anthony Perkins, M.S.
> (512)123-7890
> 5565 Cherry Orchard Dr.
> Heavenly Heights, OH 45678

Calling card format after you know your career goal.

> Anthony Perkins, M.S.
> Counseling Intern
> (512)123-7890
> 5565 Cherry Orchard Dr.
> Heavenly Heights, OH 45678

Take as many actions as necessary to keep renewing your sense of self-confidence. When it drops because of a negative event, don't let it stay there. Each confidence robbing event makes your anxiety level go up, creating an uncomfortable and self-defeating cycle.

Make a List

Make a list of things you can do that help you feel good but that don't necessarily cost a lot of money or take tremendous preparation time. My suggestions are:

Walk mid-morning every day

Invite a friend to join you for dinner at your place

Schedule time with an encouraging acquaintance

List your personal and professional assets

Set aside time each week for developing or pursuing a relaxing hobby

Write out your goals in time segments

Graph the important events in your life

Make time to be with people with whom you laugh.

Even if you aren't a morning person, the way you invest the first three hours after you get up will set the tone for the productivity of your day, so make sure they are well spent. Make a list of reasonable goals. Surround yourself with the most positive people you know, people who believe in you and your capabilities.

What If . . .?

Write a description of what your life will be like if everything turns out the way you want it to and when it will be that way. When you devise the list assume for the moment that you have no thoughts of self-limitation, no self-criticism, no past to drag around, no health fears.

Use Affirmations

Use affirmations as weapons against negative and fearful thoughts. You cannot always prevent things from happening, but you can do something about how you respond and react to life events you don't like. Does a disappointment or rebuff cause you to give up, or does it make you want to redouble your efforts and reconfirm your goals? Affirmations are:

1. Stated in positive terms

2. Expressed in the present tense

3. Specific in quantity or time

4. Reflect how good you will feel when "it" happens

5. Confirmations of when good will be in your life

Use Affirmations against Negative Thoughts

The following are examples of negative comments re-worded into affirmations.

"If at first you DO succeed, try not to look astonished."
Deep Thoughts by Jack Handley

"The future belongs to those who believe in the beauty of their dreams."
Eleanor Roosevelt

Negative

This is too hard. I know he won't even talk to me.

If I hadn't goofed off in school, I'd be OK now.

I won't be home much today, so there's no sense starting.

Affirming

I know how to request appointments in a way that recives a positive response.

This week I'm closer to knowing what I want and how to get it.

I am making five calls. My goal is to set up five Information Interviews.

Negative

Boy, she was rude.
I wouldn't call back there again if it were the last place in town.

These people never return my calls. I'll never get anywhere in life at this rate.

Generous/Confident

She must be having a bad day. I'll use a different approach next week.

OK. How am I going to place myself so I can get favorable attention from the successful people in that field?

Self-denying

Oh, I don't want to be aggressive. No one would respond well to me if I just come out and tell them I want or need their help.

Self-affirming

I am enjoying talking with the people on my contact list. I have a script and I know what to say. I can schedule appointments with them and ask for the information I need.

Due to career confusion a client found himself applying for jobs he wasn't sure he wanted. When he came to me he hadn't completed any research on potential jobs, and for his job search he was using a resume that was written in vague language that clearly said to the reader, "Please don't hire me for this job. I don't really want it. I'm only applying for it because I don't know what other choices I have." He told me that he had no choices, no network, and no direction. The affirmation I gave him to use was, "I can find meaningful work that uses my talents, in an environment where I can grow professionally." Affirmations aren't magic, they are just supposed to be reminders to help you not become discouraged, like the Wheel of Fortune described in chapter two.

Use the Affirmation Worksheet to write affirmations that address your current situation. Come back to it and use it anytime you are concerned that you can't overcome an obstacle.

"Man is what he believes."
Anton Chekhov

Affirmation Worksheet

Directions: In the left column describe a situation you are concerned about. In the second column write what you are worried about or fear. In the third column describe an outcome that you want. For example, let's say you know you want to attend an event to meet people who could give you information about one of the fields you are considering. You are nervous about meeting new people, don't have much practice making small talk, and are afraid you'll make a fool of yourself. The sample below shows how the negative self-talk is identified in the Feared Outcome column and the affirmative self-talk is in the Hopes column. When you are anxious and worried you can use this format to sort out your thoughts and make tomorrow's outcomes better than yesterday's.

Problem	Feared Outcome	Hopes
Have to meet new people and introduce myself	I won't know what to say.	I'll be prepared with my One-Minute Introduction
	I'll look foolish.	I can set a goal of meeting three people and then just relax.
	They won't like me.	I will take a friend along to sit with after the networking part of the meeting.

"But why denigrate oneself, others take care of that when necessary."
Albert Einstein

Help Someone Else

You are going to be talking to a lot of people, and you will have opportunities to help others in ways that won't take you off track too far. Start a good rumor; compliment someone.

Make it a practice of asking people what you can do for them in return when they give you information, provide professional referrals, and otherwise make your life easier. Often they can't think of anything at that moment, so tell them to "just let me know." One of the most common ways I return support to people is by being available to them. I use e-mail, write thank you notes, return phone calls, send them a copy of articles that seem relevant to their interests, and meet them for lunch or coffee.

Keep in Touch

Start a weekly (breakfast, afternoon, or evening) meeting where you share job information with other career searchers. Report on your progress from the week before and set goals for the following week. For example, fifteen telephone conversations; three information interviews set up; two hours in the library; and lunch with a former boss. Then, use the meetings to keep each other going.

One client started her own biweekly support group. She invited a few friends and asked them to bring someone. They continued to meet for over a year, talking about their careers, families, and life challenges and providing each other with a place where others would ask them how they were progressing with the goals they talked about the week before.

Do Some Mental Work

Use your sleeping hours, self-hypnosis, and relaxation exercises to accomplish your goals, face your fears, gather the courage and stamina to make the telephone calls, ask for help, meet with strangers, and call people back.

Using Your Dreams as Tools

When you go to bed at night, write down a sentence or two describing how or where you seem to be stuck. For example, "I want to meet with the owners of some hardware stores to find out whether it's something I would like to do. I want to know how to approach them." Each night, write your question until the answer comes. With practice, your answer will appear the next day. Until you learn how to listen for the answer, it may seem like nothing is happening. Stay with it. The answers will come. Watch for the changes.

A workshop participant said that she decided which networking meetings to attend each month by listing them at night before she went to sleep. In the morning one of the meetings seemed to select itself as the first choice.

Self-Hypnosis

Believe it or not, you use a form of self-hypnosis every day as you consciously and unconsciously hear the habitual thoughts in your mind. The trick is to make sure that the attitudes and recurring thoughts that you have are helping you and not harming your progress. Compare these two (self-hypnotic) thoughts:

1. "Well, I never have been able to find a good boss."

2. "Through talking to people and getting enough information, I'll find an employment situation with work that interests and challenges me, where I can use my skills and have a boss I can learn from."

A Simple Stress Reduction/Relaxation Exercise

In a quiet place, close your eyes. Put your mental attention on your physical body, starting with your head, progressing down your body, stopping for a moment to notice each section, limb, and part of you, in as much detail as you like. Regulate your breathing to the count of five, counting one, two, three, four, five, both when you inhale and when you exhale. Now you can program yourself to be relaxed when you make

"Start by doing what's necessary; then do what's possible; and suddenly you are doing the impossible."
St. Francis of Assisi

calls, to feel confident during interviews, and to remember what points you wanted to make. Imagine yourself in the situation you are fearing, and tell yourself in positive terms what you want the outcome to be. "I have the right words at the right moment. I listen in a way that allows me to find out what I want to know. No matter what comes up for discussion, I know how to respond appropriately." Notice that you are focusing on your behavior and outcomes; you cannot control the other person's behavior, only yours. Don't frustrate yourself by trying to get other people to behave the way you want them to. Your best shot is to take every opportunity to make a favorable impression and know that your centered and positive attitude will get you through whatever comes up.

Stick to the Facts

When you are feeling down about your progress, choose an uncomfortable or embarrassing situation that you have on your mind and practice separating your perceptions about the event from your feelings about it. In other words, try to describe an event that you didn't like in factual terms. Change "Nobody is returning my calls this week!" to "I called three people who do not know me on Monday. Today is Wednesday and I haven't had return calls from them." The difference in how you think about it will make a difference in what you have the power to do about it. If you have made too few calls, that's the problem.

Work Your Card File

Make it your friend. If you get up in the morning and don't feel you can focus, pull out your call sheets and your card file and look for someone to contact. Make a list of ten calls to make and start. You can always "call your mother" first, i.e., make a short call to a supportive friend who will help you get your energy going again.

A client who was having a hard time facing the phone calls made an arrangement with a friend that they would call each other before and after their ten telephone calls for the day. At the beginning of the day they compared notes on who they were calling and whether they wanted to set up information interviews, touch base with a networking contact, or identify names of potential contacts in a specific industry. At the end of the day they talked briefly about their successes and set backs, comparing what worked and didn't work.

Fear Nothing

Events that catch us by surprise are the ones which affect us the most. The embarrassing or even humiliating events that people fear and worry about the most are rarely the ones that actually occur. Think about it. It's infinitely more productive to invest in ideas that could improve your luck. Events are neutral by nature, so if you can think of them that way, your emotional state will be more buoyant.

Practice Visualization

Close your eyes and think about the times you felt successful, smart, and lucky. Remember the emotions you experienced. Use that mind-set to do what's ahead of you.

If you are worried about going to the library because you are afraid you won't know how to find the information you need, remember a time in the past when you had to do some work in the library for school. Recall how helpful the library staff was when you asked questions and how relieved you were when you found the material you needed to write that term paper.

Watch Your Diet

Antihistamines, alcohol, caffeine, recreational drugs, and sugar, in some people, can cause chemically induced depressions and make "bad" feelings harder to cope with. Only you can look at your situation and decide whether this is an area that needs attention.

Have you ever had a midnight dessert and coffee after a movie? Have you ever partied the night before an exam? Most of us can do it once in a while with little effect. More than half of my clients over the years have had to reduce their stress level in order to get back in control of their circumstances and move ahead, and for all of them, moderating what they put in their mouths during the day was part of their self-selected program.

"The harder I work, the luckier I get."
Sam Goldwyn

"Chaos often breeds life, when order breeds habit."
Henry Adams

Get Some Sleep

While not physically stressful, calling and meeting people and trying to figure out your future is emotionally stressful. You may need an extra hour of sleep at night to help you bounce back.

Dr. Alexander Clerk at the Stanford sleep disorders clinic was interviewed in May, 1994 by the San Jose Mercury News. He said that most people feel superior to nature and think that they can trade sleep for activity. Dr. Clerk points out that sleep is not a time out but is an active state that is essential for physical and mental restoration. The problems that result from a lack of eight hours sleep include the obvious ones of falling asleep at the wheel of your car and the less obvious symptoms of messing up on the job, clumsiness around the kitchen, fatigue, grumpiness, and anxiety.

Try a Different Approach

In one of his exceptional self-esteem seminars, Jack Canfield, author and workshop leader in the field of self-esteem, said that insanity is doing the same things over and over again, expecting the outcome to change. If your system isn't producing results, it needs to be changed.

Take a Chance

Risk-taking is universally acknowledged as a sign of healthy self-esteem. What have you wished you could do that would be a positive risk-taking adventure? Is this a good time to try it? (It has also been said that mistakes aren't failure, not trying at all is failure.)

Perhaps someone you know took a risk and started a second business on the side to try out a career possibility. Our newspaper reports one of these career changes almost every week. This week the story was about a woman who left a teaching career to become a tour guide. Smaller risks can be exhilarating, too. If there is a person you want to meet, call them and ask them to lunch.

Write It Down

Keep a log of your successes. Write in it compliments you have received, calls you made that you felt hesitant to make, conversations you carried well, or challenging situations you handled well.

Buy a small notebook and keep it handy. When you complete the self-assessment activities in chapter three, make a note of what you found out about yourself that you feel good about. When a co-worker says "good job" add that to your book along with the name of the person who gave you the positive feedback. As the feedback sheets in chapter two come back to you in the mail, write the most positive statements in your log.

You can look at the log and read your entries when you want to reassess your skills and when you need a pick me up. I advise everyone who is working now to keep one of these logs. If you have input into your performance review the log will remind you of many accomplishments and successes you should consider before you begin writing your part of the review. It will also jog your memory when it is time to write a resume or formulate your reasons why a prospective employer should hire you.

Get a Good Word

Ask someone you know for an acknowledgment or some praise. And, be willing to praise others, too.

Management research tells us that it takes four compliments to counter the loss of an employee's productivity from just one negative comment. In a career search and later in a job search you will experience rejections in the form of un-returned phone calls or people thinking they are helping you by telling you what is wrong with you. Seek out positive people, read your success log, and go out of your way to compliment others to balance the productivity scales in your favor.

Take a Look at Yourself

A super stress-reduction technique: Make eye contact with yourself in a mirror at close range. An advanced version: While making eye con-

"No one can make you feel inferior without your consent."
Eleanor Roosevelt

tact, say, "I like and respect you." This is one of the silliest sounding items I have here, but try it. You may be pleased with the calming results.

What Have You Got to Lose?

Sometimes you may feel like it's just not worth the effort to go through all this work, even though a wonderful, unique, financially rewarding, and personally satisfying work life will be the end result. Ask yourself, "What is more important than building my future?" As they say, "In five years, you'll be five years older whether or not you're in the same job." You may as well have that dream job or that degree when you get there.

Ask for What You Want

If you didn't get it, ask again. Ask someone else. Persistence, stick-to-it-iveness, be a squeaky wheel, or be a small stone in someone's shoe. Just don't be a thorn in someone's side.

For a more in-depth look at stress, negative thoughts, and self-talk, I recommend *Thoughts and Feelings: The Art of Cognitive Stress Intervention,* by Matthew McKay, Martha Davis, and Patrick Fanning (New Harbinger Publications, 1981).

Finally, ...

Not only expect the best. Prepare for the best and be willing to accept the best possible outcome as a result of your diligence.

"You miss 100 percent of the shots you never make."
Wayne Gretzky

Chapter 5

The Nature of the Job Market

Overview of the Job Market

A brief overview of the nature of the job market is in order so you will understand why information interviews are so important. The formal channels of job information include what you read about companies and industries in the newspaper and professional journals; the jobs your family and friends know about and tell you about; and the jobs the search firms and employment agencies know about. Those are a minuscule number compared to the possibilities that exist out there for you. There are twelve thousand to fifteen thousand job titles in the United States, and no one of these job information sources can help you beyond brief general descriptions of thousands or detailed information about a few dozen.

You know quite a lot already about the job market in your area because you notice how thick the Sunday classified section is, how many stores have "Help Wanted" signs in the window, and whether the shopping center is crowded or empty. In metropolitan areas companies rely less on the newspaper for announcing job openings and more on the internet. Since you are going to the trouble to identify the right career and job, it is important that you think practically about where you will find a position that meets as many of your requirements as possible.

The job market has a life of its own, in a way. There are job openings in some fields fairly consistently: occupations such as nursing, electrical engineering, and sales. Most workers must be prepared to change jobs and careers as economy and scientific breakthroughs alter the needs of workplaces. Typing is not used as much as computer skills are now; social service funding

"Training is everything. The peach was once a bitter almond; cauliflower is nothing but cabbage with a college education."
Mark Twain

dries up in one arena and flows to another; teaching jobs are as available in private industry as in the public system; maintaining the robots which perform assembly line functions has replaced repetitive work. Niches have opened up in environmental cleanup, growing organic produce, home cleaning services, biotechnical research, elderly and home care, and laser optics. The U.S. Department of Labor publishes *The Occupational Outlook Handbook* every two years. This source has projections about future job trends. The projections aren't always accurate or complete for your geographical area, but they are loaded with possibilities you may not have considered and are clearly worth reviewing.

Emerging Careers

A reference resource called *Big Emerging Markets, 1996 Outlook and Sourcebook* (U.S. Department of Commerce International Trade Administration, published by Bernan Press, Latham, Md., 1995) reports that U.S. exports will rise in these industries

Information technology

Environmental technology

Transportation industries

Energy technology

Healthcare

Financial services

Advanced materials

There should be job growth in those industries, as well as in the companies that provide supplies to those industries and the communities in which those industries have facilities.

Local and regional governments publish labor market information. Since government policies and government procurement drive many economies, their publications are reasonably reliable places to find out more about the job market where you want to live.

For example, in my area, Santa Clara County, Calif., three hundred employers were interviewed to determine the level of difficulty in finding qualified applicants. Here is a sample of the findings, so you know what to look for in your area. Each section includes job title, rate of job growth, how the open positions get filled, and difficulty of finding employees. Check your library or local career center or the internet for information that will help you understand what's available. Chapter six provides an abundance of sources.

Job title	Difficulty level	Hiring forecast
Assembler	No difficulty finding inexperienced workers. Some difficulty finding experienced workers.	1992: 6,460 workers 1999: 6,120 workers (note: negative growth in the number of jobs available)

Recruitment: 64% through employee referrals.

Job title	Difficulty level	Hiring forecast
Human services	Some difficulty	1992: 800 workers 1999: 1110 workers

Recruitment: Employee referrals, newspaper ads, transfers.

Job title	Difficulty level	Hiring forecast
Computer network manager	Great deal of difficulty	1992: 5,120 workers 1999: 7,140 workers

Recruitment: 64% through employee referrals, transfers, newspaper; 29% use recruiters or employment agencies.

What Kinds of Jobs are There?

Robert Reich wrote in *The Work of Nations* (NY: Alfred A. Knopf, 1991) that in the twenty-first century, the "information age," there will be three types of workers. One type of worker, the "routine producer," uses basic skills entering data into computers, processing information, and producing reports. These workers work by standardized procedures and rules, performing simplified tasks. The strengths employers look for in these workers are literacy, reliability, loyalty, and an ability to follow detailed instructions. The statistics in 1990 were that 25 percent of Americans work as routine producers. In 1995 the number of these jobs shrunk considerably.

The second type of worker, the "in-person services" worker, needs vocational training. Unlike routine producers, in-person services workers interact with the customer instead of metal, fabric, or data. In-person services workers work individually or in teams to provide cleaning ser-

"Around 50% of all white collar workers use computers today to do their jobs—up from 25% ten years ago. By 2005, the percentage could be 80."
Career Opportunities News, April, 1996

"Accept the reality of the rapidly changing workplace and think of yourself as the CEO of your own firm - YOU, INC."
Money Magazine, May, 1996, in "Here's the Good News About Jobs" by Leslie Alderman & Karen Cheney

vices to office buildings, retail customer sales, home health care, transportation, drivers and customer services, auto repair, physical fitness instruction, and administrative secretarial support. Employers require punctuality, reliability, a pleasant demeanor in the face of irritating patrons, and an air of confidence even when feeling morose. Reich states that, "above all they must make others feel happy and at ease." This is a growing category of jobs available. In 1990 the number was 30 percent of all jobs. One nursing home conglomerate employed more workers than Chrysler! It is estimated that three million of these jobs are created every year.

The third job category, "symbolic-analytic services," is work that entails problem identification and problem solving, as well as strategic brokering. The skills needed, including the manipulation of symbols, words, data, communication, design, and visual manipulation, are transferable world wide. The job titles for this category are engineers, researchers, executives, management consultants, tax and financial advisors, management information providers, organization development specialists, planners, and systems analysts. These jobs require the ability to simplify reality into abstractions and to translate complex information and abstractions into usable forms. These workers shift assets, save time and energy, innovate legal points, and manipulate sounds, words, and pictures into forms that entertain and inform clients.

Symbolic analysts are likely to work alone or in teams and usually have partners or associates rather a boss or a supervisor. In this category of jobs the income is not directly tied to the number of hours worked at tasks. Most symbolic analysts graduated from college and in 1990 were only 20 percent of the workforce. Reich points out that some job titles which sound like symbolic analyst jobs do not bear up under close scrutiny. His examples include the manager who in reality does not interact with his employees in an intellectual or mentoring role, but instead unlocks and locks the building as his primary management responsibility. Also consider educated professionals who do repetitive work for many years, such as lawyers who review wills and accountants who conduct audits.

The primary skill required of symbolic analysts is the ability to work with unidentified problems, unknown solutions, and untried means of putting them together in meaningful and useful ways, i.e. the capacity to effectively and creatively use knowledge. Thought processes and communication, not production and service, are the products for this category of worker.

The remaining 5 to 10 percent of American workers are farmers, teachers, government employees, and government contractors, all of whom are sheltered from global competition.

Which Kind of Job Will I Have in 2005?

"Only you can provide the vision, values, and leadership for YOU, INC."
Fortune Magazine, Jan., 1996, *Looking Out for Number 1* by Thomas A. Stewart

Regardless of the job title you currently hold or the industry for which you work, your ability to sustain a satisfactory work life will depend primarily on the skills you have in your portfolio. The skills that are highly valued include: problem solving, information brokering, manipulation of words, pictures, and data. Of the four categories of jobs that will be common in 2005, where have you set your sights?

1. Routine producer: Step by step tasks done under standardized procedures and methods, including the supervision of these tasks. Requirements include: accuracy, reliability, loyalty, read English.

   data entry   process information

   produce reports   production work

2. In-person services (Vocational training required) Requirements include: pleasant demeanor, confidence, make others feel at ease.

   interact with people   be part of a team

   provide services to customers

   home health care, medical technicians, massage therapists, cleaning service, driver, customer service representative, physical fitness instructor, administrative support, retail sales, taxi driver, hairdresser, security guard, waiter, child care worker, auto, home and garden repair, bank teller

3. Symbolic-analytic services (College education usually required)

   identify problems   solve problems

manipulate words   innovate ideas

design, research, entertainment specialist, consultant, financial advisor, provide management information, organization development specialist, train, coach, advise, translate complex information into usable forms and summarize reality into abstractions

4. Other workers

teacher, farmer, government employee, or contractor

Even if you complete extensive research, Information Interviews are important to an on-going process of identifying work that will suit your temperament, skills, and plans for the future. Working in industry, one discovers that there are engineers and engineers; secretaries and secretaries; managers and managers. What is meant by this is that no two organizations, agencies, or companies have identical job tasks for the same title. In fact, it is common for two people at the same company to have the same title and do totally different jobs.

Career Self-Reliance

The most frequently reprinted *Harvard Business Review* article, "Toward a Career-Resilient Workforce," by Robert Waterman, Jr., Judith Waterman, and Betsy Collard, appeared in the July-August, 1994, issue. The implication of its being the most frequently requested article in history is that its ideas have become a standard in career thinking. The primary thoughts in the article are that the days of lifetime employment in one career or for a single employer are gone forever. Everyone is required to change jobs and careers, and it is now necessary to think in terms of your employability in a variety of settings. Teamwork, community, empowerment, common vision, institutionalized quality improvement, cross training, self-management, and mutual trust are the coin of employability.

It is fully up to the worker to manage her or his career or employability in the new world of work. Workers must keep up to date through continuous learning, reinvent themselves by learning new skills, and stay flexible while employers reorganize (and reorganize again, and re-engineer, and twenty-first century themselves, etc. Dizzying!).

The rapidly changing face of the world of work means that your skills are the real currency that you have to spend and in which you should invest and re-invest. Flexibility is valuable, so you can move quickly into a new industry, move back and forth between large companies and small organizations, set up your own shop, or become an expert for hire. College grads can expect to work in seven to nine organizations, and switch industries three times during their careers. Universities around the country now offer a portfolio type bachelor's degree called "University Studies." Many college seniors are choosing the University Studies degree in order to avoid being pigeonholed by a degree in psychology, business or human physiology.

In the words of Parent Effectiveness Training, the relationship between employers and employees has changed from parent-child to adult-adult. For you, as a potential employee, there are pluses and minuses. On one hand, the constant changes make it less likely that you will become obsolete or bored. On the other hand, you must always be searching for the next right job.

Modern organizations are looking for people who take responsibility for their career success into their own hands. You are required to have an entrepreneurial attitude in order to survive.

As you move through time in a job, your skills and style change; so, a systematic and regular taking stock of yourself is recommended. At many companies, information interview databases are made available to workers who are ready to make internal job changes. The databases list other employees in the same organization who are willing to spend time with other employees to tell them about the requirements of various jobs and the nature of the work.

All of this suggests that information interviewing is a skill set that you will need throughout your working life.

"I don't believe you can really be creative and do your work if you don't doubt yourself at least once a day."
Sandra Bernhard

Chapter 6

Library Research

Objectives of Library Research

You are conducting library research to figure out what jobs you want to find out more about, how others with your interests have built satisfying careers, the names and meeting dates of associations in professions that interest you, which industries you would like to approach, what companies in your area that could help you, whom you should contact, and how to reach knowledgeable people.

Don't cheat yourself. Plan to spend from one entire day to several part days at the library. (One expert recommends that you plan to invest forty hours.) If you are working full-time and it is not possible to make that kind of investment in your career all at once, set up a reasonable schedule of shorter time periods. At the other end of the spectrum, for those of you who would prefer to spend months at the library before making that first phone call, limit yourself to two weeks of research at first. You can always go back for more. Either way, getting started is crucial.

My theory about doing at least one full day at a library is that reviewing information gives your mind and your intuition time to reflect on the suitability of various possibilities. Trying to come up with original thoughts is time-consuming, frustrating, and not nearly as productive as using others' careers as templates for yours. Compare these two scenarios. Which do you think would be the most effective and would produce the results you want?

In the first scenario, Vicky thinks she wants to make a change from first-line management in high technology to a service industry, maybe in the world of finance, such as investments management. She budgets a little time to go to the library after work on Tuesday night. Vicky is tired, but committed, so she goes anyway. The librarian helps her find the names of the five top financial planning companies, and Vicky takes the information on them and leaves, telling herself that she will contact them all within the next two weeks.

In the second scenario, Linda decides to investigate a change from computer customer service to technical writing and editing. In the course of a morning at the library, she discovers that there is technical writing in publishing, in high tech, in manufacturing, and in education. She also finds, in a directory of local networking organizations, a monthly meeting for people who do technical writing at home and one for those who do technical writing for marketing and advertising—pastures of plenty—possibilities she had no idea existed. The college catalogs reveal that a local college gives a one-year certificate in technical writing, and a local writers' group has a class on how to get started in the field. Some of this information is premature for the Information Interviewing phase of Linda's career research, but it expands her knowledge of the field and gives her more options for exploration. When she makes initial telephone calls to potential contacts, she will be able to say, "I have completed extensive library research, and I know that there are several careers that interest me and also several ways to work in those careers. I need to talk to men and women who are doing the jobs that sound like the best fit for my skills so I can make a good decision about the future."

Have you ever noticed that your mind is better at recognizing that something is right than at creating a new idea? For example, you may have noticed that some people know whether or not a word is spelled correctly when they see it written, but the same person may hesitate just spelling the word out loud. Career material is similar, in that reading about jobs, reading others' resumes in resume books, and looking through job descriptions can give your mind the jog it needs to say, "Yeah! That would be great for me, too." Coming up with an "original" idea for your Ideal Job without any input is significantly harder and more frustrating.

> "How often I found where I should be going only by setting out for somewhere else."
> R. Buckminster Fuller

Creativity and Identifying Your Ideal Job

Scientists often do not perceive accurate results and findings of their work because the solution that is presented to them is one they had never before considered. Similarly, finding your ideal career requires that you open yourself to considering solutions you have never been exposed to. Keeping an open mind during your library research requires a creative mindset. You don't have to think of yourself as creative. I'll give you the formula.

Research studies have been conducted to identify four stages of the creative process. The four stages are preparation, incubation, illumination, and validation. Each stage has specific tasks and activities for you to accomplish as you identify the career or job that fits best into your personal goals in life and uses the skills you most enjoy.

Stage 1. Preparation

Stage 1 tasks: Gather as much information as you can that is relevant to the topic you are studying.

Stage 2. Incubation

Stage 2 tasks: Take your mind off the topic by taking care of day-to-day jobs such as sending letters, relaxing with a hobby, working with the intuitive processes in chapter four, balance your checkbook, etc. Allow your unconscious mind to make associations between the results of your self-assessment in chapter three, the job market information in chapter five, and the information you find in the library. You can begin to work on your networking lists in chapter eight. Review the feedback forms (chapter two) you have received.

Stage 3. Illumination

Stage 3 tasks: Inspiration comes with an "Aha! I've got it!"

Stage 4. Validation

Stage 4 tasks: Set up a project plan (chapter seven), and conduct information interviews (chapters nine, ten, eleven).

Library research is part of Stage 1 of the creative process. Enjoy yourself as you explore new horizons.

Reference Resources

Research the companies, jobs, professions, or industries that interest you. An investment in a day or two at a business library will pay big dividends. The reference librarian of whatever library you use, whether it is a college, local, or private library, will be able to help you locate the references you need. Following is an annotated list of references that you find in most libraries.

After you research and target industries and companies, you can find more up-to-date information by calling companies and asking to talk with Public Information, Public Relations, Investor Relations, or the Treasurer's office. Most companies have printed literature to mail out, no questions asked.

Other sources of information include brokerage firms, banks, public accounting firms, and universities. Ask for a 10K Corporate Report (financial and historical information), a Prospectus (information on directors, officers, and insiders), an Annual Report (broad range of historical, financial, marketing, and product information). Look at financial information to discover whether a company is financially sound. Dun and Bradstreet is the best source of annual financial information. Every privately and publicly held company submits data annually. Dun and Bradstreet reports indicate whether or not a company pays its bills when they are due, sales records, profitability, sources of funding, etc. These reports are available through the library, through on-line internet sources, and through stock brokers. Local newspapers in metropolitan areas carry information on venture capitalization. Usually a "round" of venture capital allows for three years of job stability.

"Your library is your Paradise."
Erasmus

Federal Government Publications

The most important resources for career and job information are found in two publications provided by the U.S. Government. Most libraries have them.

Dictionary of Occupational Titles. Provides short descriptions of 12,000 jobs. Each job has a DOT code that is widely used by career services providers to research more information about the job in other resources.

Occupational Outlook Handbook. Published every other year by the U.S. Department of Labor. It is an expanded update of the most rapidly growing occupations for the nation as a whole. The editors provide a reliable resource that is reasonably accurate in its predictions regarding the world of employment.

In addition, individual state governments provide employment information by DOT codes. For example, *The California Guides* lists rapidly growing occupations by DOT code and provides a two-page description of the work, the availability, licensing requirements in California, and wages. Your state department of employment or opportunity may also provide similar information. Ask the librarian.

Employer Bibliography

Libraries feature printed resources on the labor market, industries, and companies. Use these resources to find individuals with whom to conduct information interviews. When you go to the library, the librarians are on hand to help you to identify and make use of any publications with specific listings for your geographical area.

All of the following resources are updated annually or semiannually.

Almanac of American Employers. Jack W. Plunkett, editor. (Boerne, Tx: Corporate Jobs Outlook). Lists 500 U.S. companies judged by the authors to be the fastest growing. Companies are rated for salary paid and benefits provided. Data on type of business, name of recruiter, company finances.

American Electronics Association Membership Directory (AEA). (Palo Alto, CA: American Electronics Association). Lists members by product, location, and alphabetically, including names and addresses of home office, divisions, and all officers. It is expensive so the local librarians keep it in a desk drawer. Updated annually.

BioScan: The Worldwide Biotech Industry Reporting Service. (Phoenix, AZ: Oryx Press).

Biotechnology Directory. J. Coombs and Y. R. Alston. (Macmillan Press, Ltd.). An international directory that lists products, companies, research, and organizations.

Consultants and Consulting Organizations Directory. Janice McLean, editor. 11th ed., 2 vols. (Detroit, MI: Gale Research). Contains 18,000 listings. Information includes names, addresses, telephone and fax numbers, government contract status, minority- or women-owned status, seminar and workshop titles, special services, and branch offices.

Corporate Yellow Book. (New York: Monitor Publishing Co.). Who's who at the leading U.S. companies. Company names, headquarters, revenue figures, number of employees, names of officers and senior management, U.S. subsidiaries. Also see *Financial Yellow Book,* a companion volume which lists financial services companies.

Directory of American Firms Operating in Foreign Countries. 13th ed., 3 vols. (New York: Uniworld Business Publications). Lists 3,500 companies operating in over 50 foreign countries.

Directory of Value Added Resellers. (New York: Business Guides). Lists companies that customize, enhance, or modify computers, software, or peripherals to meet specific market needs. Also by the same publisher see the *Directory of Computer Retailers.* Lists the key personnel, product lines, computer brands, network software brands, services, number of systems installed.

"Chance does nothing that has not been prepared beforehand."
Alexis de Tocqueville

Electronics Manufacturer's Directory: A Marketer's Guide to Manufacturers in the U.S. and Canada. (Twinsburg, OH: Harris Publishing Co.). Lists company and division names, key contacts, addresses, telephone and fax numbers, product information, defense contract status, employment statistics, annual sales.

Encyclopedia of Associations. Sandra Janszczak, editor. 5 vols. (Detroit, MI: Gale Research). Annual. Use this directory to identify contacts at professional, technical, social, and political organizations. A guide to 80,000 U.S. membership organizations with scope, conventions and meetings, membership, and interests.

General Career Reference

Encyclopedia of Careers and Vocational Guidance, The. 10th ed., 4 vols. (Chicago: J. G. Ferguson Publishing Co.). Industry profiles, industry outlook, career information, job descriptions, sources of additional information.

Hoover's Guide to Private Companies. (Austin, TX: Reference Press). Profiles of 500 major U.S. private enterprises. Also see *Hoover's Master List of Major U.S. Companies.*

Job Seeker's Guide to 1000 Top Employers. Jennifer Amold Mast. (Detroit, MI: Visible Ink Press). Employers are listed by state, city, industry. Information includes names, addresses, products, human resource department contacts, number of employees, how to apply, benefits of employment.

Million Dollar Directory: America's Leading Public & Private Companies. (Bethlehem, PA: Dun & Bradstreet). 160,000 public and private U.S. companies listed with addresses, subsidiaries, number of employees, SIC codes indicating primary industry, names of key officers and decision makers, profile of competitors.

Moody's Manuals. (New York: Moody's Investors Service). Identifies companies whose securities are traded, with a synopsis of size, location, products, plants, and officers. Also see *Moody's Bank and Finance* (5 volumes), *Industrial* (3 volumes), *International* (3 volumes), *Municipal Government* (4 volumes), *Public Utilities, Railroads,* and *Moody's Banks, Insurance, Real Estate, and Investment Trusts.*

Peterson's Internships Directory. (Princeton, NJ: Peterson's Guides). Information on the 35,000 listings includes names, addresses, internships available, eligibility requirements, contact information. Internship referral and placement services directories, geographic and employer indexes are in the back.

Poor's Register of Corporations, Directors and Executives. Lists 27,500 leading business organizations in the United States and Canada, including principal products, number of employees, and names of key officers.

Research Centers Directory. Anthony L. Gerring, editor. 20th ed., 2 vols. (Detroit, MI: Gale Research). Lists nonprofit and university research centers.

Standard Rate and Data Business Publications Directory. Lists trade publications in thousands of fields, by topic.

Thomas Food Industry Register. (New York, NY: Thomas Publishing). Names of companies, addresses, telephone numbers, contact names, products, sales statistics, types of customers, size of facility, number of employees.

Thomas' Register. 20 vols. (New York, NY: Thomas Publishing). Lists most U.S. companies engaged in manufacturing, by product, geographic location, and asset ratings. Display advertisements by many of the listed companies.

"...books popular with lending libraries may not always be the product of genius, but genius is not everything."
E. S. Dallas

Telephone Directories. The white pages list government agencies on federal, state, county, and municipal levels. The Yellow Pages list by products and services, names, addresses, and telephone numbers of local firms. Large libraries stock dozens of out-of-town telephone directories. Hint: Use the Yellow Pages index to look for products and services that you would be interested in working with and around.

Trade Shows and Exhibits Schedule. (Denver, CO: Trade Show Bureau). When you want to find people in a specific industry, trade shows will bring them all to one place for you.

Online Research

Research can be conducted electronically, to save time and to provide the most current information, as well as locating resources you wouldn't think of. Several formats are available for research: CD-ROM, online service providers, electronic bulletin boards, and the internet. Many directories that are available in hard copy are also available in electronic form. Using these electronic tools, you can research companies, identify contacts, read press releases, learn of new products, understand the business trends that impact an industry or a specific organization, and locate professional associations through which you can make contacts. You can also talk with others in a field you are researching, via a keyboard, to further refine your information interview questions as you gather more information.

Electronic information is updated regularly. Many CD-ROMS are updated monthly, with a two-month lag time. Online services can be updated daily or even hourly. Some resources are available from a desktop computer in your home or office. Other resources are impractical to own and should be accessed at a library. It is important to understand how to conduct an information search before you begin, especially if you are paying by the hour to use an online service. While the general process is the same, different databases use different search terms. Usually, there are instructions to guide you step by step and a help screen explaining search terms and how to refine them if the search results in too many matches to your criteria or none at all. A reference librarian is a great help when you are starting out.

Online information exists in a dynamic environment. New information and resources are added daily. Following are some general descriptions of services. Use these only as a beginning guide and be on the lookout for other useful tools.

Many libraries provide patrons access to an online catalog of bibliographic information on books, library location, and whether or not the book is checked out. Through a modem it is possible to conduct a subject search of library resources using the Online Public Access Catalog.

CD-ROM

Many libraries have CD-ROM databases which allow you to search magazines, newspapers, and other resources for information. Some databases will have an abstract of the article, some include full text, and some only a brief description. All databases list the source and date of the information so you can track down the original article if you want to read it in its entirety.

Examples of CD-ROM databases available

Info Trac (a library search tool to find company information, magazine articles)

ABI/Inform

Computer Select

Encyclopedia of Associations

Encyclopedia of Careers and Vocational Guidance

F & S Index

Million Dollar Disc

Standard and Poor's

Commercial Online Network Providers

To use commercial services, you need access to a personal computer equipped with a modem and commercially available software. You will be required to become a subscriber or member, pay a monthly fee, telephone charges, and often an hourly fee after you exceed the basic monthly allotment.

The service providers and information grow daily. Newspapers, magazines, and trade journals are available in part and selected articles are available in their entirety. Companies provide daily updates and information about their products, organizations, people, job descriptions, current openings, salary ranges, and benefits. This is all online via a telephone connection.

In addition to these databases and online corporate connections, there are forums which allow you to chat in real time or post messages and questions for anyone to read and respond to. In a chat room, you type messages on your computer and another person reads it at another location while you are typing. They type a response and you read as they type. When you post a message or question in a forum, everyone who subscribes to the forum can read all messages on the topic being discussed. You can read others' messages in topical forums and gain useful information without ever asking a question. For private messages, email is used.

A large warehouse sized bookstore I visited had over 200 books on the internet, complete with how to find a job using the internet, and lists of useful internet addresses, if you want more information than you find here.

The largest Commercial Online providers include

America Online 800-827-6364

CompuServe 800-848-8990

Microsoft Network 800-426-9400

Prodigy 800-836-1129

Bulletin Board Services

An electronic bulletin board is similar to a physical bulletin board: it's a place where information is posted and exchanged. Using a modem connection to your computer, you can read messages and participate in BBSs that specialize in a topic of interest to you, such as business, education, career, networking, professional meetings, local politics, hobbies, etc. You can read or post messages and announcements while you are online or download information onto your computer hard drive for later reading.

Municipalities all over the country have gone online, listing everything from school lunch menus to current job openings. Many are free access services, and local libraries are usually connected to them.

Lists of BBSs can be found in magazines such as *Online Access* (800-366-6336) and *Wired* (800-769-4733). *The Wall Street Journal, Investors Business Daily,* and most daily papers also provide internet references. There are books of internet BBSs three inches thick in bookstores, but it is difficult to know how current they are by the time they are published.

Most, but not all, of these information resource BBSs are free. Some require a fee to access special areas of information. Quite often you will be asked to register, define a password, and complete a user survey. The information is used by the BBSs monitor or owner, called a SYSOP (systems operator).

The Internet

This is probably the best and most challenging information resource available. The internet is actually a network of computers all over the world that are connected by relay stations. By "surfing the net" you can find statistics and industry trends, up-to-the-minute employer data, descriptions of occupations, and opportunities in any kind of work you are researching. You can probably find answers to almost anything you want to know. A few people at universities and corporations have been utilizing the internet for twenty years and are proficient at it. For most career searchers, however, it is a challenge to find information without help or taking a class.

The internet can be accessed through various sources. You can gain access through colleges and universities where you are enrolled or

"Facts, when combined with ideas, constitute the greatest force in the world."
Carl W. Ackerman

employed. Federal and state government agencies and corporations provide access at no charge. Most individuals outside those specific sources connect to the internet through a commercial online network provider as mentioned above, as well as dozens of local providers throughout the country. If you are interested in more information, how to access the internet and what it can do for you, contact InterNIC, the internet information center at 800-444-4345.

The internet and the number of providers is growing. Several monthly magazines are devoted to where to find specific information and which commercial services provide the best resources. It is getting easier to use, but it's still a good idea to begin with a knowledgeable friend, a class, or a reference librarian.

If you want to connect with the internet but don't know how, hundreds of books are available on the services available to connect with the internet. There are monthly magazines specifically geared to help you sign on, learn the basics, and find all the information and resources you need. Schools, colleges, corporations, and libraries are connected to the internet, and if you are a member or student or employee, you have free access already. Copy centers have on line services available for an hourly fee. If you decide to try one of the major providers, most of them offer a month of free service when you subscribe. There are hundreds of thousands of internet locations. The following listings were recommended by career counselors, internet reviewers, and internet writers. Enjoy!

Hot Internet Spots for Career and Job Research

General Career Research

America Online Keywords Talent Bank, Occupational
Profiles Database, Career, Jobs

Career development exercises:
http://www.adm.uwaterloo.ca/infocecs/CRC/manual-
home.html

Tomorrow's jobs: Occupational Outlook Handbook:
http://www.jobtrak.com/jobsearch_docs/occhandb.html

Career advice, resume help, job listings:
http://www.espan.com/js/js.html

Hoover's Handbook of 2,000 largest and fastest growing companies:
America Online Keyword hoover
Compuserve Go hoover.

Thousands of company reports:
Lexis/Nexis
http://www.meaddata.com

New York Times Business News:
America Online Keyword nyt Business News

Job resources on the internet:
http://www.wpi.edu/~mfriley/jobguide.htm.

Information sharing via newsgroups and mailing lists:
http://www.synapse.net/~radio/finding.htm.

Business trends for the twenty-first century:
http://www.21net.com/online/index.html

Searching the internet for career information:
http://www.excite.com/

California, Silicon Valley career information:
http://www.jobsmart.org/

Job Listings

Job listings database by job title:
http://www.adamsonline.com/

Monster Board of job resources:
http://www.monster.com/

Company profiles and job listings:
http://www.careermag.com

High Technology Careers Magazine:
http://www.careerexpo.com/

Links to job listing sites:
http://www.cs.purdue.edu/homes/swlodin/jobs.html

"A room fraught with books and people."
Fred Allen

"Abundance comes to those who have the courage to follow their dreams, to consecrate their lives to doing what they passionately love to do. This brings not only material abundance but connection with the profusion of resources, opportunities, and assistance vital to the full expression of one's talents."
George Land and Beth Jarman,
Break-Point and Beyond

Job listings from six major newspapers from Boston to San Jose:
http://www.careerpath.com/

Email listings for individuals:
http://www.bigfoot.com Bureau of Labor Statistics
http://stats.bls.gov

Searching the internet for information:
http://altavista.digital.com
http://www.yahoo.com

Thomas's Register of American Manufacturers:
http://www.thomasregister.com:8000

U.S. Census Bureau Data Maps:
http://www.census.gov/stat_abstract/profile.html

SEC listings on companies recently going public:
http://www.town.hall.org/cgi-bin/srch-edgar

Links to job agencies, by geographical location:
http://www.dice.com

Hi-tech job descriptions and job listings for contract and full-time Silicon Valley positions:
http://www.olstaffing.com

New Grads

Resources for college students:
http://www.careermosaic.com:80/cm/cc/ccl.html

College career center job postings:
http://www.jobtrak.com/

Roar - Monster Board for new grads:
http://www.monster.com:80/roar/contents.html

Colleges, career outlooks, school rankings:
http://www.usnews.com/usnews/fair/home.htm

Minority Resources

Minority employers:
http://www.BLACK-COLLEGIAN.COM/

Women's career referrals:
http://www.pursuit.rehab.uiuc.edu/
http://www.amsquare.com/america/wcenter/center/htm

Women's resources and organizations:
http://www.pleiades~net.com/lists/orgs.html

Minorities' resources on the internet:
http://www.vjf.com/pub/docs/jobsearch.html

Latino career services and listings:
http://www.hooked.net/saludos

Japanese career strategies and resources:
http://www.csinc.co.jp

"Research: the process of going up alleys to see if they are blind."
Marston Bates

Online information and CD-ROM databases are useful because they may be more current than printed materials. Online conversations can yield information exchanges with contacts that would otherwise not have been possible, if you have time and are willing. You can conduct a thorough and successful career search and find your dream job without it, however, using books, the telephone, and face to face contacts.

Use the following chart to collect data and information about at least three jobs that you can pursue. If you think you have discovered your ideal job and are ready to find out what it takes to succeed in it, proceed to the next chapter.

Library Research Results

Position Title:_____ DOT Code:_____

	Like	Ok	Don't Like
Requirements: ___Degrees, certificates, licenses, etc. ___Physical requirements			
Duties and Activities:			
Environment: ___Service, manufacturing, other ___Physical surroundings ___Location ___Commute time			
Rewards: ___Advancement opportunities ___Working conditions ___Personal satisfaction ___Salary and perks ___Co-workers			

Labor Trends:
___Growing or shrinking field?
___Emerging new products and
    services?

Related Job Titles:

Key Points:

Chapter 7

Organizing Your Project

There are as many systems of organization as there are well-organized people. Use the system you see here until you devise one that matches your research style more closely.

Index Card File

Set up an index card file (5x8) of your usable contacts, in alphabetical order. On each card, record the person's name, address, and telephone number. Make additional notes such as how they can be helpful to you or the dates of your communication and when you intend to follow-up. Add to this file on a regular basis as you recall, meet, and get leads on new contacts. Start out with a minimum of twenty-five names in your file of people you plan to approach, taken from your Brainstorming List. Use the back of the cards for notes to yourself that help you remember who the individuals are.

If you were doing an actual job search, you would probably build up a file of two hundred to five hundred names: fifty to seventy-five recruiters and employment agencies, thirty friends, fifteen to thirty former co-workers, ten to twenty professional association acquaintances, and thirty names of professionals you identified through library research and newspaper articles. For this project you may have more or fewer names depending upon how quickly you make your career decision, how difficult it is to break into a field, and how much time and energy you have to make contacts. Keep these cards even after you complete your current efforts. Hopefully, you will be able to contact them again in the future about your progress, and you may decide to send them holiday cards in December to express your appreciation for their support. In addi-

tion, when a friend gives someone your name as a contact bridge, you'll be ready to give back to the network.

You can keep the cards organized alphabetically by company name or by contact name, or you can put in a set of monthly date separators and file them by the date you are planning to make your next contact. If you maintain them alphabetically, you should keep notes in a date book or on a calendar by who you are to call and meet with that day. Cards in a box are the method I prefer, because on the days when it seems like you aren't getting anywhere and nothing is happening, you can thumb through the cards and make some calls. Date books or notebooks do not act as a ready reference. (Salespeople call the file indexed by date a "Tickler File," by the way.)

Planning and Scheduling

The project plans used by corporations to ensure the timely completion of every aspect of a project are essentially time-lines that are sketched out in pencil and reviewed by the participants to be sure the goals are attainable. (Setting goals *that can be reached* is the mark of a successful planner.) Anyone who has worked from one of these plans knows that Murphy's Laws interfere with the accomplishment of some of the items, so slippage in the schedule (when things don't happen as soon as they should), while frustrating, is to be expected. The Project Plan Chart on page 85 shows how you might fill one of these out.

Assign a specific block of time each week to plan your research (Sunday evening and Friday afternoon seem to work especially well), to review the week you just ended, and to plan your activities for the following week. Monday morning doesn't work well for most people.

The Activity Chart on page 86 shows how to list the specific number of each activity to do (five calls to known contacts, for example) and the optimal and minimum amount of time to spend doing each (half an hour optimum; fifteen minutes minimum, for example). Under the Actual column you would indicate how much time you actually spent.

Project planning also requires that large tasks be broken into their component parts so that you have attainable and measurable goals. The Tasks Chart on page 87 shows you how to define your tasks. Your major tasks will include items such as library research, company research, letter

CONTACT CARD

Referral Source: _____

Name:_____

Telephone #: _____ Fax #: _____

Title:_____

Company Name:_____

Address:_____

_____

Notes:_____

_____

_____

_____

Referrals received

Name	Title	Telephone #

> "For a system to remain alive, for the universe to move onward, information must be continually generated. The fuel of life is new information-novelty-ordered into new structures."
> Margaret Wheatley, *Leadership and the New Science*

- -

CONTACT CARD

Referral Source: _____ _____

Name:_____

Telephone #: _____ Fax #: _____

Title:_____

Company Name:_____

Address:_____

_____

Notes:_____

_____

_____

_____

Referrals received

Name	Title	Telephone #

writing and resume revisions, scheduling information interviews, and attending networking meetings related to the jobs and fields you find interesting. Don't forget to keep a contact record to keep track of your telephone calls.

You can use the blank forms on pages 88–92 to begin your project plans. You may want to make more copies of these or just use blank paper to structure your own.

Example Project Plan Chart

Start date: _____ Projected completion date: _____

Tasks	Week 1	2	3	4	5	6	7	8	9	10
Library	●		●		●		●		●	
Brainstorm contact list	●	●								
Call people I know for names		●	●	●		●		●		
Find network groups			●		●		●			
Attend network meetings			●	●	●	●		●		●
Send letters requesting Information Interviews			●	●			●			
Go on Information Interviews (3/week)					●	●	●	●	● ●	
Re-work contact lists					●	●		●		●
Coffee/lunch (1/week)		●	●	●	●	●	●	●	●	●
Telephone calls DAILY			●	●	●	●	●	●	●	●
Follow-up letters					●		●		● ●	●
Follow-up calls			●		●		●		●	

You can see that if you draw one of these on a large sheet of paper in the area where you are organizing your search, you could write in your goals in pencil, track your progress, and build in corrections. It helps keep you on target, and for some people, reaching the goals adds fun to balance out the work.

"As for conforming outwardly, and living your own life inwardly, I do not think much of that."
Thoreau

Example Activity Chart

The block of time I will set aside to make my weekly plan is

_____

Sample Weekly Plan (for week of _____)

Goals:

	Plan A	Plan B	
Activity	Optimal	Minimum	Actual
_____Calls to known contacts	_____	_____	_____
_____Calls to new contacts	_____	_____	_____
_____Face-to-face Info. Intv.	_____	_____	_____
_____Lunches and dinners	_____	_____	_____
_____Networking meetings	_____	_____	_____
_____Hours researching new options	_____	_____	_____
_____Letters mailed to new contacts	_____	_____	_____

People I met with this week:_____

_____

One item essential to complete this week:_____

_____

The one person I must reach:_____

The next person I want to meet with or identify to talk to will be someone whose job is this interest area:_____

Notes:_____

_____

_____

_____

_____

_____

_____

_____

Example Task Chart

10/4 Major Task: Make 5 new contacts in field I'm exploring by 10/14.

To Do	By (date)	Completed
Call 5 contacts and ask for names	10/9	_____
Make list of known contacts	10/4	_____
Find their phone numbers	10/5	_____
Write to out-of-town professor	10/6	_____
Clear off desk	10/4	_____
Buy stationery and stamps	10/4	_____
Write telephone script	10/5	_____
Practice script on friend	10/6	_____
Start calls to new contacts	10/7	_____

"You must do the thing you think you cannot do."
Eleanor Roosevelt

"Planning is to bother about the best method of accomplishing an accidental result."
Ambrose Bierce

Project Plan Chart

Start date: _____   Projected completion date: _____

Tasks	Week	1	2	3	4	5	6	7	8	9	10

Activity Chart

The block of time I will set aside to make my weekly plan is
_____

Sample Weekly Plan (for week of _____)

Goals:

	Plan A	Plan B	
Activity	Optimal	Minimum	Actual
_____	____	____	____
_____	____	____	____
_____	____	____	____
_____	____	____	____
_____	____	____	____
_____	____	____	____
_____	____	____	____

People I met with this week:_____
_____

One item essential to complete this week:_____
_____

The one person I must reach:_____

The next person I want to meet with or identify to talk to will be someone whose job is this interest area:_____

Notes:_____
_____
_____
_____
_____
_____
_____
_____

"Action is transitory, a step, a blow, the motion of a muscle—this way or that."
William Wordsworth

Task Chart

Major Task: _____

To Do	**by (date)**	**Completed**
_____		
_____		
_____		
_____		

Task: _____

To Do	**by (date)**	**Completed**
_____		
_____		
_____		
_____		

Task: _____

To Do	**by (date)**	**Completed**
_____		
_____		
_____		
_____		

Contact Record

Company Name _____

Address _____

Contact Name _____

Title _____

Telephone _____ **Fax** _____

Date Contacted _____

Result _____

- -

Company Name _____

Address _____

Contact Name _____

Title _____

Telephone _____ **Fax** _____

Date Contacted _____

Result _____

- -

Company Name _____

Address _____

Contact Name _____

Title _____

Telephone _____ **Fax** _____

Date Contacted _____

Result _____

"There are two kinds . . . in one's life—people whom one keeps waiting and the people for whom one waits."
Samuel N. Behrman

To Do: Calls to Make and Letters to Send

Name	by (date)	Completed

Chapter 8

Building a Professional Network

Networking is a System of Contacts

Networking means creating a system of contacts both for information and for support. It links you with others who can help you and whom you can help later, if not now. If you do not have a network, you begin by joining with others who share common interests with you. For this project you will be seeking out individuals who know about a career in which you have an interest. Over time, your network contacts can include people who share other interests as well. With attention, your initial leads from your career search can become the basis of a widespread network of contacts, as you each cross-introduce each other to more like-minded and interesting acquaintances and friends.

Networking is not using people. Initially, it may feel like you are only receiving, but as you gather information and build up your list of contacts, you will have opportunities to help others. After a few conversations, you will find that you too have knowledge that others want to hear about. Then you will be giving as much if not more than you are getting.

The hard part of networking (which every person in sales encounters and has to confront) is the fear of rejection and the occasional "casual" handling by others, i.e., the perceived rejections. In sales training, trainees learn that, on average, only one out of ten people will buy. It's not a hard and fast rule, but it's a place to start. To get ten "yes" responses, the rule of thumb is to make one hundred presentations to potential buyers.

OK, you aren't selling; you are looking for information and twenty minutes of time for a face-to-face conversation. So, that improves your odds of getting what you ask for to at least 50 percent, maybe to 90 percent. Your approach will make all the difference. If you are being rejected repeatedly, your approach is the problem, and you should rewrite your script entirely. If your telephone script isn't working more than 50 percent of the time to gain information interviews, telephone contacts, and referrals, go back to the script-writing instructions and begin fresh (see chapter ten).

The critical thing you need to know about networking for information interviews is that networking will always be with you: you will need it for promotions, future job searches, and finding peers in your field for continued professional development. Learning the how-to of building and maintaining a professional network is fundamental not only to getting the right job but also to your long-term success as well.

For some people the most challenging part of building a network is their fear of meeting new people. Getting to know yourself and what it takes for you to walk into a room where your task is to introduce yourself to strangers can make you feel shy and awkward. Sometimes when introverted, shy people introduce themselves to me they say silly things or stumble over their words. I don't judge them because I know that it is their discomfort speaking and that I, too, stumble when I am trying too hard to make a good impression.

Overcome your initial discomfort through preparation. Write one or more versions of your One Minute Introduction (instructions are in chapter ten) so that you have something memorized to pull you through when you can't think of what to say.

When you call an organization's representative to find out where and when their meetings occur, ask her if she will be attending the meeting. If she is planning to attend, tell her that you would like to meet her when you arrive. If she isn't going to attend, ask who usually helps new members become acquainted and how it's best to get started meeting people. Usually there is a membership chairperson who will greet you and introduce you around.

At the meeting, use your One Minute Introduction to ask her to point out whom you should meet. Maybe she will introduce you. Nothing makes friends more quickly than a shared enthusiasm about an interest. I assume that if you are attending a meeting of people who are passionate about preserving historic buildings, for example, it's because you share their interest. Most of your anxiety is because you are thinking about yourself. Think about the job, career, or topics that are the focus of the meeting, tell people why you are there and what excites you about the field and then ask them what their primary interest is. Now you have a conversation going. Ask them if they know of anyone in the association who shares your particular interest, and if so, would they be willing to introduce you.

If you are afraid you'll forget why you're interested in their work, take along some of your notes from your library research and try to get people interested in helping you resolve the questions that remain in your mind about the field or an opinion piece you read in a professional journal.

You may have some conversations that fall flat. I usually recommend that clients go with a goal of starting three conversations or of finding two people who will give them a referral or useful information. With a finite goal in mind, they feel less like they have to charm everyone in the room.

Take a friend with you and then go to one of their networking events with them. When you go to their meetings, explain to people that you accompanied a friend who is researching career possibilities and is excited about their field. Ask them how they happen to be in that career and what their special interests are. And, by the way, you can practice your One Minute Introduction at your friend's meeting and look for contacts, too.

The joy of networking is the longtime friends, job-hunting buddies, support group, lunch partners, future bosses, and sometimes even sweethearts you will meet. You will hear about good restaurants, wonderful vacation spots; good, bad, and ugly employment situations to run toward or to avoid; books and movies others are enjoying. You won't feel alone any more in your circumstances. Take a few minutes now to do test your networking IQ on pages 101–103.

> "The meek shall inherit the earth, but not its mineral rights."
> J. Paul Getty

Networking Quick Facts

1. Your most valued contacts over time will be people you like and enjoy being with who have interests in common with you.

"The rule of my life is to make business a pleasure and pleasure my business."
Aaron Burr

2. Some people you are not particularly fond of, but who you respect nonetheless, can help you. Previously hated bosses and co-workers sometimes become supporters when asked.

3. The best contacts are at the top of the pyramid, i.e., general managers, regional managers, division directors, vice-presidents, CEOs (chief executive officers), CFOs (chief financial officers). They have information, they can delegate an information interview to an appropriate person, and they are conscious of being the public relations voice for the company.

4. The best time to reach executives is before 8:00 AM and after 5:30 PM.

5. Join one mixed group in your profession and one all male/female group for the best coverage of concerns and topics.

6. When choosing between two networking organizations, go for the ones that are most positive and uplifting in their membership and presentations.

7. Examine your network by noting who you call regularly and with whom you lunch. Intentionally expand your contacts with a system.

8. Know your goals in networking. Who are you trying to meet? What are you hoping to discover?

9. Bring topics and news to talk about. Prepare to contribute.

10. Everyone wants to look good to their friends and business associates. When you call or meet with a person whose name was given to you, treat that person with respect whether or not they are interesting to you. Otherwise you could lose two contacts.

11. Always have as a primary goal making a friend, rather than getting something from someone. Even if the person with whom you talk does not have information right now that would help you, if they like you, they will think about you when they hear about openings in other organizations and may even make a

few calls on your behalf.

12. Devise a system for maintaining regular contact with people, even if you only have enough time to make a ten-minute call or jot a "thinking of you" note on a postcard. Put a reminder on your calendar. As isolated as many of us feel in our depersonalized society, you know how much it can mean to someone that you thought of them.

13. Give back to the network by remembering to pass on information that would interest someone you met. Send them copies of writings: an article in the paper on a topic they are concerned about or chatty news about a competitor. Send a copy of complimentary press coverage to someone who spent time with you or helped you.

14. Expect it to take thirty to one hundred days to build a results-producing network from scratch.

15. Your attitude is the most important asset you will need, and the second most important asset is your personality.

16. For people who use the networking method to find a job, here are the typical outcomes, indicating that personal contacts work

225 resumes sent = 1 offer

2 personal contacts per week for 12 weeks = 1 offer

17. Simply said, networking is an effective way to find promotions and lateral moves within your current company, to change companies or careers, to enter the job market for the first time, or to reenter it after an absence.

How To Build A Contact List

When you call your previous co-workers, networking contacts, an uncle, a golf partner, or bridge club buddy, it should be clear that you do

"Letting people in is largely a matter of not expending energy to keep them out."
Hugh Prather

not expect them to be the answer to your research for the ideal job. Instead, approach them in a way that does not put pressure on them; for example, "I need the support of your knowledge and experience. I'm not sure you can give me the advice I need, but you may be able to suggest someone who can."

A career search client told me that during an information interview the person he contacted said, "I'm not any good at 'networking' and I don't know anyone, really." Because my client said, "That's OK, please just keep your eyes and ears open for me," she relaxed and asked, "Well, what about so-and-so who works at XYZ Co.?" Of course, it was a very good lead.

With prompting, your contact could remember that she met a marketing manager at a Rotary lunch who seemed to know everyone in the field you are investigating. Even if it seems like a long shot, take the name and telephone number and call the contact. In your call to the marketing manager you'll say something like, "_____ gave me your name because I need some advice. You may or may not be able to help me directly, but _____ said that you may know someone who can." Friends have relatives, relatives have friends, and almost anyone can give you a name or two. Write letters to the ones you feel too timid to call or who seem too distant to call.

Find the names of three professional organizations in fields that interest you. Newspapers in towns and major cities list meetings for the week or month, and business newspapers like *The Business Journal* in metropolitan areas list networking events. The reference librarian will refer you to books that list organizations locally and nationally. The Chamber of Commerce often publishes and tracks professional organizations. Your goal is to locate the meetings in your area by calling local chapters and writing to the national headquarters. Go to local meetings—up to three a month if you have the time—and talk to people, tell them you are thinking of a career in their field and ask what they think you should know about it and with whom you should talk before you pursue it in earnest. Take notes. Ask if they know someone else you should talk to before deciding on a career direction or changing careers. Lots of people will try to discourage you from entering their field either because you look like competition or because they don't like the work any more. Don't let it discourage you. You'll be five years older in five years, whether you are a carpenter or a fisherman. If it takes five years to get into something you really want, so be it.

Here's another salesperson's method of gaining contacts. Make a list of

1. People you would like to meet in a particular industry,

2. Names of companies where you would like to make contacts,

3. Job titles that interest you.

Carry it with you, especially when you go on information interviews, attend networking meetings, or meet with friends and family. When you are talking with someone, ask him, "Here is a list of companies I am considering contacting. What do you think of them?" or "I have a list of people I hope to meet during my research, how do you think I could best approach them? Have you ever heard of any of them?"

If she or he reacts favorably to a company, ask, "Do you know Mr._____, the Vice President of Finance there?" or "Do you know someone who works with them?" If the answer is yes, you have the referral you've been looking for. If the answer is no, ask, "Do you know anyone there whom you would suggest I contact?" Even if the contact doesn't know anyone at the company personally, you could still call your target company and say, "In a recent conversation with Mrs. Black, the Vice President of Marketing at Xegar, your company was discussed as one I should talk to in the process of researching my ideal job." That kind of opening provides a conversation bridge that gives you more confidence and makes the person you are calling much more responsive to you.

I worked with a client who identified what he wanted in terms of career progression in the commercial construction industry. David was fairly successful in his current company, but knew that he would not be able to advance because it was a family owned company and all the top positions were permanently filled by family members for generations to come. David used the library's newspapers on microfiche to find as many possible companies and potential contacts. Then he asked everyone he knew in the industry and the companies who supplied them if they knew anyone on his list.

"If A equals success, then the formula is: A=X+Y+Z. X is work. Y is play. Z is keep your mouth shut." Albert Einstein

As he found links into other companies he met them for coffee. In this way he identified the one company that was a match for both his career goals and his personal values of working for only highly ethical organizations. Armed with thorough research on the industry, he called the president's secretary and made an appointment to talk with him on the telephone. During the phone conversations, David explained that he had researched the industry and found that the president's company was the best in terms of customer satisfaction, ethical business practices, and employee recognition. The president was suitably impressed and agreed to a dinner meeting. Two rounds of interviews and three weeks later, David was working for his number-one choice. His research paid off not only in increased income but he also has a more interesting position and works with good people he enjoys.

Building Your Initial List

The nature of brainstorming is that it is a noncritical thinking process, so the initial lists you'll be making aren't to be limited to individuals who you think have jobs that you want. Anyone on this list could know someone who knows someone. Use the chart on pages 104–105 to jot down each person who comes to mind in the category, creating a long list to be weeded out and re-worked later. It doesn't matter whether or not you like each other. You may usually say, "Oh, I don't know anybody," or "I really don't have friends." But for this important task, take the positive approach, "I'll think until I have one name in each category." Everyone you can list here knows at least as many people as you do. Think of the number of potential information that is out there waiting for you.

Test Your Networking IQ

Before you begin building your networking list complete the following quiz to see how well you understand networking.

Instructions: Place a "1" in the Yes or No column that best represents your current situation. The scoring and interpretation information follow the quiz.

	YES	NO
1. Do you have a system in place to track your networking contacts, for example a Rolodex, card file, or computer spread sheet?		
2. On a weekly basis, do you contact at least one individual in your network who is outside your daily work environment?		
3. Have you contacted each person in your extended network at least once this year?		
4. In the last six months, have you reviewed your network and decided what types of contacts you need to cultivate?		
5. Is there an individual in your current network whose advice you could get regarding the requirements of a job that interests you?		
6. Have you researched any new career possibilities for yourself during the past year?		
7. Within the past eighteen months, have you discussed at length a different career possibility with a person who holds a job you may want later in your work life?		
8. Among your personal acquaintances, is there anyone whose job interests you as a possibility for your future?		
9. Have you called someone you do not know within the past year to discuss his or her career?		

"Good order is the foundation of all good things"
Edmund Burke

	YES	NO
10. In the last six months, have you sent a note congratulating a professional in your field for his or her accomplishments?		
11. In the last three months, have you sent a thank you note to a professional who helped you?		
12. In the last six months, have you written to a researcher whose work interests you or to an author whose work stimulated or amused you?		
13. In the past nine months have you sent a copy of an article to a peer or mentor?		
14. Do you have monthly lunch appointments with people who could be key to a future job?		
15. Do you participate in professional organizations?		
16. Within the last year have you participated in community, education, or religious organizations?		
17. Are you an active member of any groups outside your field of work?		
18. Do you keep up to date with periodicals and new thoughts in your field?		
19. If you were put in charge of a meeting on a topic in your field, would you know who in your network you could contact to pull the meeting together?		
20. Do you attend conferences related to your current field or another field that interests you?		
21. Do you make a point of meeting new people when you attend conferences?		

	YES	NO
22. When you meet new people who talk about their professions, do you know what to ask them to find out if it is a field that would interest you?		
23. In the last month have you contacted a new acquaintance to stay in touch?		
24. Do you discuss others' career goals with them and help them whenever you can?		
Totals	**YES**	**NO**

Scoring Instructions: Add the number of YES responses and the number of NO responses. How successful are you at building and maintaining a network? Read below what your total YES score indicates about your current level of networking.

Interpretation

17–24 points in the YES column: You understand the importance of networking. You have a good chance of reaching your career goals.

10–17 points in the YES column: Your score points to being a good networker. A little more follow through will increase your opportunities for future career success.

0–10 points in the YES column: It's time for you to focus on building and sustaining a network. The tips and tools in this book will make you a much better networker and will help you more than someone who scored higher.

Individual Items

Items 1, 2, 4, 17, and 20 cover some basic building blocks of a network.

Items 5, 7, 8, and 9 are actions you can take to identify helpful contacts.

Items 10, 11, 12, 18, 19, and 22 encourage you to locate people outside your field who can help you define your goals.

Items 13, 14, and 15 focus on your current position level. These are the minimum.

Items 20, 21, and 22 suggest that you use professional conferences to build your network. When you go, set a goal of meeting new people and talking to them about their jobs.

If you scored 10 or below the next chapter is for you. In it you will begin to build lists of people you know as a way to develop a networking list.

"The truest wisdom ... is a resolute determination."
Napoleon I

Contact List

Friends:

Name   Occupation

_____

_____

_____

_____

_____

_____

Co-workers, both present and former:

Name   Occupation

_____

_____

_____

_____

Bosses, supervisors, managers:

Name   Occupational Industry

_____

_____

_____

People you met at conference meetings, charity drives, club activities, in formal and informal organizations:

Name   Where you met

_____

_____

_____

_____

Spouse's boss and co-workers:

_____

_____

_____

_____

Relatives:

Name   Occupation

_____

_____

_____

_____

Insurance agent: _____

Clergy: _____

Realtor: _____

Neighbors: _____

_____

Lawyer: _____

Doctor: _____

Dentist: _____

Classmates: _____

_____

_____

Roommates: _____

Acquaintances: _____

_____

_____

_____

Teachers, Professors, Instructors, Principal, Mentors:

_____

_____

_____

_____

_____

Others on your holiday card list:

_____

_____

_____

_____

New networks to build (e.g., meet a hotel manager, an architect, a technical writer, or whoever else you think you should meet in order to get where you want to go):

_____

_____

_____

_____

_____

_____

_____

"Nothing great was ever achieved without enthusiasm."
Emerson

Chapter 9

Contacting Target Individuals

Written correspondence has some advantages over prospecting for contacts by telephone. Some industries are more conservative than high tech and prefer a letter to arrive before your call. You will also have the advantage of mentioning your correspondence when you follow up by telephone. A previously mailed letter allows you to say, "I wrote to Mrs. Magnanimous last week and am calling to discuss my research with her. She is expecting my call."

Whether you are telephoning or writing letters for research interviews, keep in mind that your communication will mention the specific reasons for these contacts.

1. You are planning to change careers and want to find out about other jobs where your skills, education, and experience would be an asset.

2. You have researched current information from libraries and industry sources and are ready to speak to experienced people in the field to fill in the gaps before you select a job search focus.

3. You are new to the area and need to find out everything you can about the industries here before you move into an all-out job search.

4. You have, after considerable exploration, decided on a field and would like feedback on your resume and on how realistic your goals are.

5. You have always thought that your talents lie in a particular field and need to find out what some of the avenues are for entry into it.

When you ask for information and help, appeal to the person as an expert. It is important to show interest. The comparisons that follow provide examples of how to change your wording to make it more appealing to the reader.

USE	DO NOT USE
Your industry is particularly interesting to me.	I'm just looking into everything right now.
I would like help in choosing the course work that would complete my education in your field.	I'm not good enough in math to excel in purchasing.
Your company came to my attention as the leader in the industry, and I want to talk to the leaders.	I heard you were hiring a lot of people right now.
I was successful in the work I chose for my first career, and I want to carefully research this next move.	I never was really happy with my job choices.
I've left manufacturing after 25 years and am researching the next opportunity that would utilize my skills and management experience.	I finally got out of the rat race and was hoping that owning a franchise yogurt shop would keep me from going crazy with extra time on my hands.

Letters

Letters should be letter-perfect. A friend, secretary, teacher, career counselor, job-search buddy, or spouse with a good eye for grammar and correct letter form should review them before mailing. You should invest in good quality paper (cotten content paper may cost an extra .05 per sheet) and find a typewriter or word processor to use or to rent. (Libraries and colleges often have typewriters, and copy centers rent word processors by the hour.) If your handwriting script is good, a handwritten letter is very appealing to people who read typewritten material all day. If you write "Personal" on the envelope, that may help get it delivered to the person you're planning to see.

If your address is stable, you could invest in some personal letterhead stationery. If you're good at the word processor, you can make a letterhead—just your name, complete address and telephone numbers, centered at the top of the page in a clean type—and run it off on good paper at a copy center using your own paper. It's an inexpensive and quick alternative to printing costs.

"You have to take life as it happens, but you should try to make it happen the way you want to take it."
David Campbell, *If You Don't Know Where You're Going, You'll Probably End Up Somewhere Else*

"Apt words have the power to assuage the tumours of a troubl'd mind."
John Milton

The content of the letter is, of course, what's most important.

Read your letter out loud. A letter should sound natural and clear. Let the reader know how you got her or his name or happen to be writing to him or her, who you are and what you want, and tell them when you will contact them. Any information you can put in the letter that compliments the person on their good professional reputation lets them know that they are important to you. Commenting on the excellent reputation of the company or on some detail about their products and industry indicates that you did your homework. It's human nature to prefer to talk with people who have interests in common with us.

The Eight Keys to Successful Letters

1. Use a positive approach

2. Tell the person how you got his or her name

3. Make it clear who you are

4. Explain what you want

5. Describe how he or she could help you

6. Specifically state when you will call for his or her response

7. Cordially thank the person for his or her help

8. No matter what, make the follow-up call when you said you would

Research enough companies, contacts, and associations at a time that you can send out at least five letters in each mailing. That discipline will prevent you from waiting and hoping that the one you sent is "the one." There isn't just one job title for you, and there isn't just one job out there for you. There are clusters of suitable jobs and several companies that could employ you. Make your research broad. You will narrow it when you have enough information to begin a job search. This is still an information-gathering phase and is somewhat a numbers game.

Tom, who works in a manufacturing company, sent out five letters the first week. He was enthusiastic and committed to his career project. Then his life became busy with family responsibilities and his commitment to coaching Little League softball, but he followed up on those initial letters and identified three more leads. Tom thought things would "fall into place" and did not have a plan in place for sending additional letters. When those initial three leads did not yield useful information, his initial momentum had run its course. He had to start all over again and build up to approaching more contacts.

Another client, Mary, had worked ten years as a bookkeeper. When she started her project, she made a plan to prepare five letters every Sunday night. On Monday, Tuesday, and Wednesday of the following week, she called the people whom she had not been able to reach the week before, and on Thursday and Friday she initiated follow-up calls to the new contacts.

After three weeks of regular follow-up, she met with two people whom she met through this process of making contacts. Her project was interrupted because of a move to a different house, but she missed only one week of sending letters. Even though the move kept her busy, she made time to return any calls that came in. Mary's biggest concern when she began sending letters was that she found it difficult to ask for help from others. After a month she realized that asking for help could yield good results. She said, "It's been astounding to me that once I let down my guard and stopped trying to look perfect all the time, that people really wanted to help me."

Six Openings and Bridges for Correspondence

1. "Your reputation as a civic leader often quoted in local publications has prompted me to seek out your advice on a personal matter."

"The great aim of education is not knowledge, but action."
Herbert Spencer

2. "As one of the top executives in the field of _____, your expertise in what it takes to succeed in your industry must often be sought. Would you meet with me to give me the benefit of your guidance?"

3. "Because of the outstanding reputation of your company, and its leading position in corporate security, your advice would be most valuable to me at this time."

4. "Ever since we worked together on the school fund raiser, I have thought that your advice would be valuable to me when it was time to resume my career."

5. "I have no expectation that you have a position at Sterling Plastic Corp. for me. However, your comments and advice about the future prospects in the industry as a whole are what I need."

6. "Within the coming months I plan to begin a new career in sales. Your name, Ms. Wonder Woman, was given to me by Mr. Big as someone who is knowledgeable in the field."

Sample Letter to New Contact

Your Name
Your Adress
City, State, Zip
Today's Date

Mr. Billy Blue
Manager, Research and Development
V-Rad Corporation
42 Main Street
Missoula, Montana 69882

Dear Mr. Blue:

In my desire to find a good job fit for my skills and experience, I have researched several career path options and industries where I am confident I could make a contribution. This summer I will graduate from Local University with a degree in physics and would like to talk to professionals working in the field to discover exactly what the jobs are like.

Your name was in a very interesting article I recently read on physicists working in the Missoula area, and I am writing to you in the hope that you will be able to help me either by spending half an hour with me or by referring me to someone in the area you would recommend.

I will call you within a week to arrange a meeting or to get your advice for a referral. I understand that you are busy and appreciate your help. I look forward to talking with you.

Sincerely,

(your signature goes here)
(your name typed goes here)

"Who cannot give good counsel? 'Tis cheap, it costs them nothing."
Robert Burton

Sample Letter to Someone You Discovered Through Research

"In mathematics there is no difference between "The glass is half full" and "The glass is half empty." But the meaning of these two statements is totally different, and so are their consequences. If general perception changes from seeing the glass as "half full" to seeing it as "half empty," there are major innovative opportunities."
Peter Drucker *Innovation and Entrepreneurship.*

Your Name
Your Address
City, State, Zip
Today's Date

Name
Title
Company
Address
City, State, Zip

Dear Mr. _____:

Your name came to my attention while researching the field of _____ as a possible industry where I can help a company reach its goals by using my skills and experience.

At this time I am exploring a variety of professional positions to discover the ones that would be the most appropriate focus for my attention in a job search.

I will complete my bachelor's degree in electrical engineering next June at (University) and am using these months to plan ahead for that time. The course work for the degree has led me to believe that there are several possible directions my career could take. During the summers between academic years, I have worked at (Company) doing _____, which I found very interesting.

Based on your knowledge of the field, you could help me considerably by discussing the kinds of jobs you know about for a recent engineering graduate with my experience.

Within the next week, I will contact your office to arrange a convenient time for our meeting. I know you are busy and will keep our conversation to 20 minutes. Thank you for your consideration.

Very truly yours,

(your signature goes here)
(your name typed goes here)

Note: Center the letter on the page, with a little more white space on the top than on the bottom. Don't send a resume at this time, you will use it as a reason for future contact. Don't use all your ammunition for contacts at the first meeting.

Request for Information Interview, with Contact Name

Your Name
Address
City, State, Zip
Today's Date

Ms. Linda Pastoral
President
The Peaceful Group
2311 Graceway Lane
Honolulu, Hawaii 88888

Dear Ms. Pastoral:

In a recent conversation with _____, Director of Marketing for Extron Mining, he suggested that I ask you for advice.

Although I am currently employed, I am looking for new ways to use my talent. (Contact Name) _____ assured me that because of your experience in the field, I should not move ahead with my career plans until I discuss my ideas with you.

I would very much appreciate an opportunity to talk with you. I will call your office to request an appointment, in the hope that we could meet for twenty to thirty minutes sometime next week.

Very truly yours,

(your signature goes here)
(your name typed goes here)

Note: You should follow up on this letter within forty-eight hours, before it gets lost in a stack of papers or delegated for a form letter response. It may take two or three calls to schedule an appointment. Don't give up if you really think this person can help you. If it turns out that she cannot, ask her to recommend someone who can.

"We never learn anything by means of gradual improvement. We advance by sudden jerks and abrupt starts. Then we may remain stationary for a few weeks, or even lose some of the proficiency we have gained. Some people, not realizing this fact about the way we progress, get discouraged and abandon all effort. If they were to persist, if they were to keep on practicing, they would suddenly find that they had lifted like an airplane and made tremendous progress again overnight."
Dale Carnegie

Casual Notes

"Words are loaded pistols."
Jean-Paul Sartre

Dear Barbara,

I need your advice and some straight talk about what it's like to be a supervisor in the textile industry. I'm thinking about a career change and have always valued your perspective. I'll call to set up a time to talk that's convenient for you.

Yours truly,
(your signature goes here)

Dear Jon,

It's been a quite a while since we had time to play golf together. I'd like to get together soon to get your advice on a career change I've been considering. How about the 23rd? I'll call to confirm.

Sincerely yours,
(your signature goes here)

Dear Mitch,

Help! I'm graduating this summer and would really like to talk to your dad again about the jobs at his company. We had a good talk over the holiday at your house, but I'm not sure how to reach him about scheduling time for an information interview. I'll call next week to get your thoughts and his number. Thanks.

Sincerely,
(your signature goes here)

Dear Hillary,

It's been months since we talked! I'm ready to talk to you now about what you do as a fashion designer, how you got your first job, and what it's really like out there.

The boys are old enough now that I am ready to seriously look around for possibilities. I'd like to hear your feedback, too, about where you think I would fit. How about a long walk a week from Sunday? I'll call you to set it up.

Yours,
(your signature goes here)

Sample Letter of Introduction to Someone Who Was Referred, with Contact Name

Your Name
Address
City, State, Zip
Today's Date

Ms. Lilly White
Personnel Manager
Cornerstone Property Management
1122 Diamond Street
Crystal, Tennessee 32265

Dear Ms. White:

George Helpful suggested that I contact you about my long-term interest in working in personnel management in Tennessee. He told me last week that you were someone who would give me "straight information."

Since I will be in Tennessee on a business trip in a few weeks, I hope that you will be able to spend a little time with me to give me some advice.

I plan to follow-up on this letter with a telephone call to your secretary to establish a telephone appointment. At that time we can talk about the dates of my trip and your availability. I could really use the benefit of your expertise and knowledge.

I look forward to our telephone conversation and to meeting with you in April.

Yours truly,

(your signature goes here)
(your name typed goes here)

Note: Letters, resumes, and telephone scripts are alive, meaning they will continue to change, improve, and smooth out with experience. Let them change, and plan time to change them. (The Tibetans say that all human troubles come from resisting change. Don't resist.)

"A man's language is an unerring index of his nature."
Laurence Binyon

A Letter of Introduction about You to a Referral

Date

Mr. David Woodzig
78 Maple Lane
Orange, CA 12345

Dear Mr. Woodzig:

During the last four years, Jim Allen has worked part-time for Treetop Trimming as a trimmer, customer service representative, and sometimes bookkeeper. We have appreciated the quality of his work, his dependability, and his willingness to get the job done.

Now that he is completing his education, he is ready to work full-time in a job that utilizes his education major, which is accounting. Jim isn't sure what kind of position he wants, and I would like to help him get the professional advice he needs. From our conversations, I thought that you would be an excellent contact for him.

I took the liberty of giving Jim your name and number, and he will be calling you soon to arrange an information interview appointment. I trust that you will find time to meet with him.

Thank you for your help.

Yours,

Harry Treetop

Thank You Letters

Thank you letters consist of the following four parts:

1. Compliment the person's knowledge, expertise, help-fulness, company.

2. Define how he or she helped you.

3. Thank the person for the lead, mention when you met the individual they referred you to, and what you gained from the meeting.

4. Mention that you will keep them advised of your progress as your search continues.

"Every word is a preconceived judgment."
Friedrich Nietzsche

Thank You after Information Interview

(Take the person's name and address information from his or her business card or call the company to verify it.)

Your Name
Address
City, State, Zip
Today's Date

Name
Title
Company
Address
City, State, Zip

Dear Ms._____:

Thank you very much for taking the time to meet with me Thursday to discuss professional growth possibilities in _____ industry. I was impressed by your knowledge of _____ and appreciated your insight regarding the ways I can use my skills to contribute to _____.

You gave me the name of _____ at _____, and we have an appointment early next month when she returns from a business trip.

I will be in touch from time to time to keep you informed on my career research and will bring a copy of my resume to your office as soon as it is ready. Thank you for your help and the valuable information.

Sincerely yours,

(your signature goes here)
(your name typed goes here)

Chapter 10

What to Say on the Telephone

When you call a company to arrange information and research interviews, there are some common telephone hurdles and blocks to overcome. Telephone blocks are put up to screen out calls that are unnecessary or potentially irritating. The person screening calls is doing a job. Be prepared with good answers to typical blocking questions. Following are some common telephone hurdles.

1. What to say to the person who answers the call

2. How to talk to the secretary or administrative person who screens calls for your target contact

3. What you should say when you must leave a message

4. How to explain your quest to the target person in a way that makes him or her willing to set aside time for you to discuss your future career plans

5. Your emotional reactions to short-tempered, confused, busy people who can challenge your self-confidence

6. What to say to the targets who turn you down

7. What to say to the targets who say yes

Following are some suggestions for overcoming telephone blocks.

If he /she says this	**You can say this**
What is this about?	I'm following up on a letter sent last week. Is she in?
Does he know you?	Yes. May I speak with him?
She is out.	Do you know when she will be returning calls?
He is no longer with us.	Who replaced him in that position?

If your target person says this	**You can say this**
I'm busy.	I know it's your busy season. I'd be happy to meet with you after hours or before 8 AM any day next week. What day could we get together?
I don't think I can help you.	Whom on your staff would you suggest I contact?
We aren't hiring.	I'm not looking for job openings at this time. I want your advice only. Could you give me 20 minutes at 4:00 next Thursday?
Call Personnel.	Since I'm looking for advice about what types of jobs there are in advertising, I need to talk with someone who is working in the field. Who would you recommend I contact?
Send your resume.	Can you schedule a 20-minute appointment with me in two weeks, say, Friday morning at 9? I will have it by then and will bring it with me.
We just had a layoff and - we aren't hiring.	I heard that. Your business experience is the only topic I'm interested in right now. How about meeting with me next week?

Telephone Scripts

Telephone scripts are very helpful when you are first starting out or are nervous about contacting people. Having a plan of what you want to say—and practicing it so that it comes out sounding natural, not rehearsed—helps in making a good impression on the person you're talking to. The following scripts are my idea of what works, but I'm not you. You have your own vocabulary and your unique way of speaking that's comfortable, so you'll want to write a personalized script. In addition, industries have their own languages. If possible, practice your telephone scripts with a family member or a friend or your dentist or somebody familiar. At a minimum, practice in the privacy of your room (bathroom?). Some of us do better diving in with both feet, with our eyes closed. If you are at your best just forging ahead, then use your scripts on the telephone only after you have read them aloud to yourself twice—but make those calls to companies that are not your number one or number two choices.

"Man's speech is like his life." Plato

Writing Your Script

Use one of the following examples to write a telephone opening script that describes your situation, so you can practice it before you reach your target persons. It will change with use, but here's a hint: the most successful salespeople use a script and stick with the one that works the best for them.

Hello, my name is _____. Do you have time to talk for a few minutes? *or* Is this a good time for you to talk with me for a moment?

I [was given your name by] [found your company through] [know that you are an expert in] _____.

Currently I am arranging information interviews with _____

and I would like to meet with you _____.

Or try this version

Hello, my name is _____.
I would like to follow up on a letter I sent last week. Is this a good time to talk?

I am calling to arrange an information interview with you to discuss_____[industry, jobs, or professions].

I would like to meet with you one day next week. Do you have half an hour next [Thursday afternoon] _____?

Verify the address, date, and time before you hang up. Sometimes the addresses in the telephone directories are for administrative buildings and your contact person may be in a different one. If you forget, you can call and ask the operator or receptionist for the information.

Please be aware that the people you call are not obliged to help you in any way. Thank them for what they give you. On the other hand, some people you meet over the telephone and in person will not be helpful and will be unpleasant about it. Eighty percent of Americans say they don't like their jobs, and you may have just talked to one of them. Hang in there, that's not your fault. Take a break and then make the next call. Don't end a day of calling on a sour note. If someone's response gets to you, make at least one more call. It's like getting right back on a bicycle after falling.

One career client I worked with found a way to get through a day of phone calls without being affected by the attitudes of other people. Gail was determined to make contact with ten people a day. On a piece of scratch paper she kept track of the number of calls she had to make to reach those ten. She separated the calls into two categories, helpful people and monkeys. Each time someone was rude, she put a mark in the monkey column, and when someone was pleasant, she put a mark in the helpful people column. At the end of the day there were more marks in the helpful column, and it pointed out to her that even though rude people seem to impact us intensely, they are in the minority.

Another slant on information interviews was provided by ENCOM-PASS on America OnLine:

> We propose what we call creative conversations. The purpose goes beyond collecting information. The primary focus is on building relationships. It is the connection and relationship you have with people that offers the greatest opportunity.
>
> The creative conversation is a context for synergy—a means of establishing a quality of communication so that the result is greater than what was available to everyone before the process began. It is a journey as well as a vehicle for discovery and invention.
>
> It requires more of an entrepreneurial attitude and clarity of what you want to gain out of the conversation. In the creative conversation, expectations are discussed up front and follow up is required afterwards. Also, you leave the meeting with names of others from the person you met with that are interested in doing the same thing as you want to do.

All of this implies that you are prepared before you call, by utilizing all of the steps included here, from research to follow up.

Ten Telephone Networking Contact Courtesies

1. Ask if they are free to talk right now.

2. Tell them you are doing a network campaign as part of your career decision research and that you know that talking with people in a variety of fields is the only way to find out what the jobs are actually like.

3. Say that you are looking for names of people who might know of professionals in _____ industry doing _____ kind of work.

4. Politely explain that you'd like to arrange a time to meet at their office or tell them you'd like to call back

"Discretion of speech is more than eloquence."
Francis Bacon

to get a name of someone who: works for certain industries; has worked for a company in a field you're looking into; represents a company in the industry; competed with one of these companies; works for a company not on the list but in a related field; or has a contact at one of your target companies.

5. Ask when they would be free to discuss your research further.

6. Call back at the appointed time.

7. Take the names you are given with phone numbers and company names and tell them you would like to be in contact again if appropriate.

8. Ask your friends to introduce you to their contacts by phone, letter, or in person.

9. As a conversation bridge and to help the person you are calling identify you, ask if your "friend" has called about you yet.

10. When you are given a contact name, send them a note saying that you appreciate that, and that when you called, their friend was helpful (or whatever). If they could not think of anyone to refer you to, your note will say that you appreciate their talking to you and that you will contact them again in case they think of someone who has the kind of experience, job, career, or contacts you need.

Your One-Minute Introduction

To cover yourself in a telephone interview (or in professional association meetings, or other unexpected—but important—opportunities to talk with people) you should prepare a brief introduction to yourself. Your one-minute introduction should cover enough basic information about you to let the listener know who you are. Following are two examples:

Example #1 "I'm from Kansas City, Missouri, originally. After graduating from high school, I attended college at Iowa State University and majored in English Literature. During high school and college, my favorite classes were in journalism. I worked on the school paper and the yearbook in high school and the paper in college. Since then, I have worked as a typesetter and as a columnist for a small-town weekly paper where I am now editor. The jobs I've been thinking about would be a career change, into either technical writing, marketing, or insurance sales. So I want to get as much information as possible before moving ahead. I need the name of someone to talk with who actually does technical writing. Do you have any ideas for me?"

Example #2 "My most recent position was in public relations and sales, representing a public television station to the business community. I wrote press releases to keep the station in the public eye, supervised the organization of several successful fund-raising events such as the opera night they hold every September, attended the station board meetings to present proposals and results, met with corporate representatives (primarily CEOs and members of Boards of Directors) to define the benefits of providing the station with financial support. I enjoyed the work so much that I decided to broaden my experience in PR and am now looking at the possibility of a position in a corporation or a public relations/advertising firm that would build on my experience base. I'm investigating the kinds of jobs available in those arenas. Do you know anyone you think I should talk to in order to find the information I need?"

Once you have the details of your introduction jotted down, practice saying it. Rehearse ahead of time to make it easier and more natural for you to respond to the question, "Tell me about yourself." And, when you go to professional association meetings in a field that interests you, there will be many opportunities to talk with people who are sincerely interested in you.

"In doing we learn."
George Herbert

Write Your One-Minute Introduction

Hello, [my name is] *or* [I'm] _____.

They'll say,

How do you do, my name is _____.

Chitchat, then they'll either ask you or you will create an opportunity to say your one-minute introduction. (In networking meetings, these are often referred to as a "One-Minute Commercial.")

Most recently I have been in _____
[industry] *or* at _____ [school].

I was there for the last _____ years.

My interests are strongest in _____
and so now I'm looking for information
about_____ and would like to meet
people who _____.

Do you know anyone like that, or do you have advice as to how I could connect with someone who knows someone?

The One-Minute Introduction technique can be used as a method of facilitating an effective exchange of information in groups. I have used it to help individuals obtain networking leads and information in groups ranging in size from six to two hundred. If you are a member of a career development or job search group, I recommend that you try it.

Basic Instructions: I provide a five-by-eight-inch card for all participants and make sure everyone has a pen or pencil. There must be enough room for people to stand and move around, as they change partners for the sections of the activity.

Step One: Each person writes the first line of his One-Minute Introduction, stands, and uses "Hello, my name is _____" to introduce himself to any person next to him.

Step Two: Next, each person writes out the second sentence, "Most recently I have been _____. I was there for the last _____ years." and then practices saying it to one person sitting or standing nearby, preferably not the same Step One practice partner.

Step Three: (This part of the introduction takes a little longer to write. Be sure to allow enough time for all the participants.) Everyone writes the next section, "My interests are strongest in _____, and so now I'm looking for information about _____ and would like to meet people who _____. Do you know anyone ———————?" Each participant will practice this with one other person. Then, ask the group if they have any questions. Respond to their questions, and then have them practice Step Three a second time.

Step Four: Instruct the participants to stand in small cocktail party type groups of four or five people whom they do not know well or have never met. Each person in turn will practice his entire One-Minute Introduction to the group.

The goal is to get the names of people in specific industries, positions, and jobs. A friend of a friend may know that person. Everywhere I have used this method, participants have received leads. Even in a group of five people who had never before met, one man received a lead that yielded a job offer. In an outplacement company group of thirty-five participants, eight participants received names of contacts and leads. In the group of two hundred, there was so much enthusiasm and information flying around that most people left energized.

When arranging your information interview, I strongly recommend that you make an attempt to meet your target contacts in their office. If they don't have time, accept an information interview over the telephone. You want to meet in their office because

1. Usually their contacts' addresses and telephone numbers are there.

2. You will get a better sense of the work by being in the surroundings.

3. Books and references important to researching the field will be readily available on their bookshelf.

4. The meeting is to be arranged at their convenience, and often that means that you go to them.

"What we have to learn, we learn by doing."
Aristotle

"I know how to listen when clever men are talking. That is the secret of what you call my influence."
Sudermann

Now let's take a minute to review what we've covered so far.

An Example to Recap Research Methods and Telephone Interview Techniques

Let's say that our friend Virgil Young has discovered that his personality, style, training, and natural skills make him especially well suited for the electronics industry in research and development engineering, working in a company that has fewer than two hundred employees on staff. A small company environment suits both his willingness to do a variety of tasks and his distaste for organizational bureaucratic layers. Now what can he do to find out what jobs to shoot for and where they are?

1. Go to the library.

2. Talk to friends, family, contacts, former bosses, instructors, etc.

3. Ask parents and relatives about their friends' jobs and companies. Make lists of people to contact. Write letters and make telephone calls. Set up interviews.

4. Read the want ads in the Saturday/Sunday large want ads section and the want ads in the Tuesday Wall Street Journal. He is looking for trends, company information, general business information—not job openings. This is still a learning phase.

5. Go to the career counseling and placement office at the high school, local junior colleges, or university and ask for information, guidance, and help.

6. Visit local resource centers.

When Virgil went to the reference section of the library, the reference librarian pointed out the directories that list local companies by size, industry, and location. During his library research for target companies, he found that there are twelve electronics companies in his area that employ under two hundred people.

He listed them in his contact record.

Contact Record

Company Name Source Systems

Address 14430 Cole Road, My Town 67890

Contact Name John Dear

Title Vice President of Engineering

Telephone 555-9876   **Fax**

Date Contacted

Result

- -

Company Name Magnemight, Inc.

Address 8723 Shady Lane, My Town 67899

Contact Name E.N. Bean

Title Vice President of Engineering

Telephone 555-3672   **Fax**

Date Contacted

Result

After listing the possibilities, Virgil called Mr. Dear's office, putting the date of his call on the "Date" line. After the call, he noted the result on the "Result" line for future reference.

Virgil Makes a Call

OPERATOR: "Source Systems."

VIRGIL: "Mr. Dear's office, please."

OPERATOR: "One moment."

MR. DEAR'S ASSISTANT: "Mr. Dear's office."

VIRGIL: "Hello. My name is Virgil Young. Could I please speak with Mr. Dear?"

ASSISTANT: "I'm sorry, Mr. Dear is out of the office. Could I take a message?"

VIRGIL: "Yes, my name again is Virgil Young. My telephone number during the day is 555-1234. I am a senior at Local University, and during an in-depth research of the companies in the area that I would like to work for when I graduate, I discovered Source Systems. Since Mr. Dear is the Vice President of Engineering, I hoped he could direct me to someone who could discuss the kinds of jobs that exist in the field of engineering with me sometime soon."

ASSISTANT: "Have you sent in your resume, Mr. Young?"

VIRGIL: "No, I'm not ready to submit resumes, yet. I am researching jobs and career possibilities in the area to find out more about engineering jobs in general before I actually begin to job hunt. Do you know when Mr. Dear would be available to call me?"

ASSISTANT: "He will be in this afternoon. I'll give him your message."

VIRGIL: "Excuse me, I didn't hear your name."

ASSISTANT: "I'm Marsha."

VIRGIL: "Thank you very much, Marsha. I will wait for his call."

NOTE: If you say you will wait for his call, you must. A telephone answering machine is a very useful job finder's tool, if it works and works well. No rock and roll music, children's voices, clever innuendoes, or laugh tracks on the message tape, please.

A note about the person who answers the phone: 1.) You have no idea who it is. It could be the Human Resources Manager who just grabbed the phone, the C.E.O.'s spouse, or other individual significant to your goals. Please assume that all people are significant to your future and should be treated with respect and care.

2.) My secretaries have gotten more than a few people in to see me by saying, "This person is SO nice and really wants to talk to you." On the other side, they have put message notes on the bottom of the stack, saying, "Oh, I don't know what s/he wanted," or worse, "That guy was a jerk!"

IDEAL SITUATION: Mr. Dear has the time and the inclination to call Virgil shortly after lunch. (He has the time to call because Mr. Dear is not on his way out of town to see a customer, or is not getting ready for an urgent meeting, or otherwise legitimately too busy to return the call immediately. You cannot afford the luxury of taking it personally when people do not return your calls. Taking business situations personally uses up a lot of energy that you need for other activities.)

Virgil answers the phone: "Hello, this is Virgil Young."

MR. DEAR: "Hello, Virgil. My assistant tells me that you are interested in discussing engineering opportunities at our company."

"How forcible are right words!" *The Bible* Job 6:25

VIRGIL: "Thank you for taking the time to call me. Actually, Mr. Dear, I am graduating this June and have been researching the kinds of jobs a new grad can expect to find. My reading has included a lot of interesting jobs, but I want to know more about what they are by talking to professionals in the field. Whom in your field would you suggest I talk to?" [An individual investigating a career change would say she was exploring new ways to use her skills. A reentering home executive would say something like, "I have been working at home for the last fifteen years and would like to explore ways of using my efficiency and organizational abilities in the private sector."]

MR. DEAR: "Well, Virgil, I admire your serious approach to this. Tell you what, I'll have you talk to my Director of Manufacturing Engineering. He's been around the field and is a member of a local engineering professional association, so he's familiar with more kinds of jobs than I am at this point in my career. His name is Howard Fine. Why don't you call him and arrange some time with him."

VIRGIL: "May I tell Mr. Fine that you gave me his name?"

MR. DEAR: "Oh, yes. Please do. You can reach him at 555-6888."

VIRGIL: "I would like to call you again if I need other information that I think you could provide."

MR. DEAR: "Okay, Virgil, but I think Mr. Fine is your best bet. Good luck now."

VIRGIL: "Thank you. Good-bye."

Immediately, Virgil puts Mr. Dear's name on his To Do list to send him a thank you note within two days. He puts the information about Mr. Fine on his contact list. He calls Mr. Fine now to arrange a time to meet with him.

You can see that a prospecting call or an advice call is simply a normal conversation, like the ones you have when you call a store to gather information before you purchase something. Your goal is to establish rapport by being polite, considerate, and asking direct and reasonable questions.

Always conclude the conversation with a comment or question that leaves the door open for you to contact the person again. Mr. Dear and Mr. Fine may become part of Virgil's permanent professional network.

Commitment

In *The Fifth Discipline* (published by Doubleday, 1990) author Peter Senge identifies three levels of involvement. They are Commitment, Enrollment, and Compliance. Commitment is characterized by "I will it. I will do it." Enrollment implies, "I want it to happen. I will work within the existing system." Compliance is an attitude of "I'll do what you ask." Your targets want you to come across as representing Commitment and Enrollment. Even if you have to leave a voice mail message, communicate through your words and tone of voice that you are committed. Whether you are talking to Ms. or Mr. Helpful over the telephone or in person, the way you describe your situation makes a difference. Notice the differences in the attitudes reflected in the following comparative statements.

Commitment: Fully responsible for making something happen

"Hello, Joan. I need a few minutes to talk to you. Is this a bad time?"

"Hi, Jim. This is Homer, again. Sorry we have to keep leaving voice mail messages, but you're the contact George Zest said I had to talk to before I make a career decision. When you call back let me know a good time and place we could meet next week. I'd be glad to come to your office, meet for coffee, or take you to lunch. Your choice."

Compliance: Going through the motions

"Oh, uh, hi. I'm supposed to ask you some questions about your job."

"Hello, Maggie. My name is Naomi Push, and I'd like to know how you got started in your career, who your customers are, and how much you make. I think I'd be good at what you do. Call me back and tell me when I can come to your to your office."

Success is that old ABC—ability, breaks, and courage."
Charles Luckman

"Mrs. Success Story, this is Ms. Iwanna Career. Your name has been mentioned in almost every article I have read in the professional press about women who started their own business. I have a vision of starting a business that would help my community. I'm just not sure that it's feasible and I'd like your input. Could you help me with an hour of your time?"

"Miss Valorious, I hope you will help me. You see, I want to see if I can talk you into giving me a hand with a project I'm hoping to get off the ground. It's like this, I know you're one who could make this happen and I don't know who else I can ask. I'll do whatever you tell me needs to be done."

Chapter 11

What to Say and Do
on an Information Interview

Basic Guidelines

By now you have set up appointments, so it's time to prepare. The following guidelines may seem basic or simplistic, but go ahead and read them as a refresher.

1. Dress for the job you want, or a little better. When in doubt, pants are out for women, ties are almost always suitable for men. Three-piece suits are worn in very few companies, but may still be required and therefore required to make a good impression in some industries, such as finance. If you have time, you can drive by the company at starting time, lunch, or quitting time to observe the employees as they enter and leave the building. Notice whether they wear business casual or dress more formally. Are women dressed conservatively or fashionably? Are the men dressed in suits or wearing shirt sleeves.

   For example, a finance executive I know was chastised by an interviewer for wearing a blue-and-white-stripe shirt instead of a bright white one. In another example, a software engineer was criticized for wearing a colorful tie with his suit because everyone in the company wore jeans and hiking shoes. When I was a recruiter, candidates sometimes asked before they came in whether the environment was casual or formal, whether a suit or tie was customary. It's okay to explain that you want to dress appropriately for

the environment. Ask for information from the person who sets up the appointment.

2. Be on time, or a few minutes early. Please do not arrive more than fifteen minutes early. If you do, park nearby and read the book you brought. Find a restroom and check your grooming.

3. Balance is a challenge—be polite, not stiff or too casual. "No, thank you" to an offer of coffee makes an infinitely better impression than, "Nope. I never drink the stuff."

4. Some topics are too personal. No comments on the food habits of others, messy desks, spots on their clothing, the rude comments the receptionist made, family illnesses, or your evaluations of other companies or interviewers. Never never make negative comments about a previous employer, even if the interviewer prompts you to do so.

5. Be friendly. Most of the people you meet will be genuinely interested in talking with you and making you comfortable. However, this is a touchy topic for some professionals, because they aren't sure of themselves, so it's your job to help them be comfortable with you. Avoid sexual banter—even if they start it, you can refocus the conversation to a more relevant arena by saying, "About the new products, Mr. Dodge, which one did you say your division has responsibility for?"

6. Wait quietly and patiently after you greet the receptionist. Count backwards from one thousand if you are nervous and want to squirm or smoke. Ask the receptionist for company literature. The company magazine, industry newspaper, or recent annual report is often on hand. Or take something to read with you in a folder, or sit and write positive affirmations about your great conversational skills.

For example, you should already have a pad of paper or a notebook with you for taking down information, and you can use it to jot down your thoughts or the questions you want to ask. Making a grocery list

could relax you. One time I wrote a letter to my
mother while I waited for an interview.

7. Invest in yourself and in your future by having your
   suit pressed, your hair and beard neat, your shoes
   soled and polished. Dark socks and shoes for men;
   neutral color hosiery for women. Check your hands
   and nails; bathe; handbag or briefcase should be
   clean and not bulging; avoid garlic and onions; wear
   little or no cologne or perfume. (By the way, many
   clients have found perfectly fine interview suits in the
   clothing resale shops at very low prices. Lots of the
   items available are new or nearly new, especially in
   the consignment shops.) You don't have to buy in a
   fancy store to ask the sales personnel for interview
   clothing advice. In this week's career column in the
   San Jose Mercury News, Sherrie Eng, the career
   writer, headed a column with, "Leave your baggy
   pants, miniskirts and do-rags at home." Maybe at
   your last job you didn't have to dress up, but you
   don't want that job anymore. You are asking this individual not only for advice, but also for the names and
   telephone numbers of people he knows personally
   and professionally. Make it easy for them.

8. Practice your handshake so it feels natural to you. By
   custom, men always shake hands, but women can
   also offer a handshake, especially in a business setting. Usually the professional you are meeting will
   set the tone and offer his or her hand. If this is
   unusual in your experience, you can walk toward
   yourself, extend your right hand, and say, "Hello.
   Thank you for taking the time to see me," in front of a
   mirror. Then practice shaking hands with people you
   meet. If your hands perspire quite a bit, carry a hand-
   kerchief, which you will use before you meet the
   person. Then wait until they offer their hand. Handshake or not, greet the interviewer with, "Hello, Mr.
   Big. I'm Ms. Career seeker. Thank you for taking the
   time to meet with me."

"A place for everything...and everything in its place."
Henry G. Bohn

How to Get What You Came For

Since you will meet with people on information interviews only after you have conducted some research on the company, on the industry, and maybe even know something about the career of the person you want to interview, you are going as an informed and interested party—you will be irresistible to almost any human being you will meet.

Prioritize what you want and need to know as a result of the interview, so that you are focused in your questions and get the information you are there for in a mercifully short time. In most business situations, it is infinitely better to be thought of as someone the contact would like to talk to again than as someone who just seemed to stay and stay. As the axiom in show business goes, leave them wanting more.

You've completed some homework, so you know what's important to you: you've identified your strengths, enthusiasms, skills, and interests, even if you aren't sure where or how you would like to apply them.

By the way, please don't go on information interviews with the hidden agenda of a job interview. Most people will see through your plan, and you will not necessarily get what you need, which is cooperation, advice, support, and referrals.

You may want to take a folder with a few sheets of paper for taking notes or an attache case, if you are comfortable with one. Ask for correct spellings of names of secretaries, names, titles, company names, and telephone numbers of the contacts you will be given.

Three Last-Minute Reminders

1. Observe, listen: Within reason, let them do the talking.

2. Take a few of your business cards (three to five in pocket or purse).

3. Make the most of the time you have: Stay on the topic.

What to Ask When You Are There

So what do you want to know from these generous people who have set aside time to help and advise you and who, hopefully, will give you the names of some business friends and acquaintances?

Your practice interviews have given you a sense of what your friends and relatives say in response to questions. Your research has opened up some areas of interest. Reading the company's annual report made you curious about an aspect of its growth. The experience you had on your last two assignments gave you reason to think that there is something more interesting out there for you. What do you want to find out about this person's occupation that would help you know whether or not it is for you?

You will note that the style of most of the questions I am suggesting are "open-ended" ones that encourage the individual to speak at length about her or his field. Open-ended questions begin with the words, Who, What, Where, When, How, plus, What do you think . . . .?, Would you describe . . .?, Which classes, journals, . . .?

Fifty-Two Sample Questions to Ask and One Question That You MUST Ask Every Time

Rewrite up to ten of these that suit your interests and the possibilities you are exploring

1. I'm fascinated by the field of motorcycle racing and would like to know how most people get into the field.

2. How did you become interested in winery ownership?

3. What do you think is the best educational preparation for a career in marketing management?

4. Which part of the job is most challenging for you?

"Men learn while they teach."
Seneca

5. Is there enough growth in the computer resale business that you would advise someone like me to get into it?

6. The banking industry has been going through dramatic changes in the last five years. What have you seen from inside Bank of the World?

7. In your experience, what are the dangers of truck driving?

8. Of all the individuals you have met in police work, what personal attributes do you think are essential to success?

9. How often are there layoffs in the semiconductor plants? How does it affect the morale of your employees?

10. Where could I write to get up-to-date materials on CPAs working in Big 8 firms?

11. Which professional journals and organizations should I know about in organic gardening?

12. I would like to walk through and see with my own eyes the areas where your newspaper is actually printed. Can that be arranged?

13. What are the qualifications you look for in a junior manager?

14. Which clothing manufacturer has the best track record in promoting women into management?

15. As far as you know, which software companies hire and train the most recent college graduates?

16. What skills are required of a Chief Executive Officer on a day-to-day basis?

17. What do you think of the experience I have had so far, in terms of getting into public relations?

18. What experiences have you had that you think have been invaluable to your learning the business?

19. Which classes would you recommend I take before I go any further?

20. How did you get your job?

21. From your perspective, what are the problems in working for the nonprofit sector?

22. Would you describe a typical work day in the life of a motorcycle racer for me?

23. What motivates you to stay in spite of the difficulties of political life?

24. When would my earning potential begin to improve if I chose a career as a life insurance agent?

25. Many consultants have told me that it is lonely to work that way. How do you combat the loneliness of self-employment?

26. How often do you work past 6:00 and on the weekends?

27. How many years of apprenticeship does it usually take to get a paid position as a disc jockey?

28. How well do you think I would fit in a college drama department with my background?

29. I have about $10,000 to invest. How does that compare to the average guy who wants to launch a print shop and see it through to being profitable?

30. Who do you know whom I should talk to next in hospital administration? When I call him, may I use your name?

31. What else do you think I need to know in order to make an intelligent decision about elephant training as my career?

32. What is the reason most people give when they leave dentistry?

"Questioning: Man's finest quality."
Solomon Ibn Gabirol

33. What would you say are the life-style considerations of outside sales?

34. Regarding promotions, how quickly have most managers risen to the top in the home furnishings business?

35. What industry experience do most of the directors on the Board have in common?

36. If you could do it all over again, would you choose the same path for yourself? Why? What would you change?

37. Considering what you know about my skills, education, and experience, what other fields or jobs would you suggest I investigate before I make a final decision?

38. From your point of view, what qualities do you look for in personnel managers?

39. Who are the most important people in internal medicine today?

40. In which seasons of the year do problems seem to multiply on a chicken ranch?

41. What positions would I now be qualified for in corporate training?

42. Which of my skills do you consider strong points in administrative work?

43. What do you see as the real product of the legal profession?

44. How does your company compare with the others we have discussed?

45. What is your response to my resume? How would you suggest that I change it?

46. Do you foresee developments in waste management that will affect future opportunities?

47. What training opportunities do you think I should expect in an entry-level job?

48. Have you noticed that it is necessary to change companies in order to advance?

49. Is there a trend toward an overabundance of people entering the software development field?

50. Where do you see the opportunities for self-employment in parts distribution?

51. Are there other job titles that I should be looking at that are comparable to technical writer?

52. What types of positions has your company recently hired reentering women into?

On every Information Interview, ask some form of:

Can you suggest anyone else whom it would be helpful to talk to?

May I use your name when contacting her?

Some Obstacles You May Encounter during an Information Interview and How to Handle Them

Silences: Refer to your list of open-ended questions.

Rude responses: This person is probably very busy. Thank her and leave early if necessary.

Lengthy answers: Occasionally you will meet with a person who has a lot to say. If you are benefiting from the information and have time, let them talk. If their conversation isn't relevant, refocus the interview by referring to not wanting to take too much of their time and asking another question on your list.

"Creative minds always have been known to survive any kind of bad training."
Anna Freud

They fall into interview mode: Restate that your goal is information only.

If it becomes a job interview: Assure your contact that you aren't quite ready to zero in on a job. However, if the job sounds like one you would like, find out as much as you can about the position he is describing and ask if you can see him in the next week or so for another conversation about it. Arrange a time to meet again.

Debriefing

When you leave an information interview appointment, or even complete a telephone conversation, your impressions at that moment are the most valuable ones for learning. Take debriefing notes immediately after you leave the office or location of an information interview, or you could use a small tape recorder for recording your thoughts after the interview. Ask yourself questions similar to the following, and record your answers on tape or paper for later evaluation.

Debriefing Form

Company _____

Products _____

Name _____

Title _____

Name of secretary/assistant _____#_____

Job titles discussed _____

_____

Contacts she/he gave me:

Name	Title	Tel #

1. What impressed me most?

2. What made me uncomfortable? How could I have changed this?

3. Who led the interview?

4. How did this person become successful?

5. What advice did s/he give me about my career and research?

6. Where did s/he suggest I get more information?

7. How did the conversation change my opinion about the jobs I have been considering?

8. What problems are there in this industry that I can solve and would like to help solve?

9. In what ways would this person be a good mentor?

10. What else could I have asked? What would I change if I could redo the interview?

11. What, if any, information did I agree to send to this contact person?

12. What's next? Who should I contact next?

Overall impressions:

_____

_____

_____

_____

_____

_____

_____

_____

_____ Date the thank you letter was sent

Chapter 12

Making a Decision

What Now?

Congratulations! You have completed a research process that will contribute to your success and happiness for many years to come. You are ready to sort out the hundreds of bits of data you have collected and make a good decision.

You have asked yourself the right questions, completed your research, attended meetings, and conducted information interviews. Yet it seems like you haven't found "it," the career or job that makes you sing and dance. Or, you have found three jobs that sound like getting paid for having fun doing just about everthing you hoped for. Now what?

If nothing appeals to you as your dream job, it's possible that you do not have enough experience or the right kind of work experiences that allow you to know your capabilities. You will have to choose the job that seems best. Go after the closest fit for your current ideal job description. Work, learn, listen, participate, watch, network.

To oversimplify thousands of books a bit, consider the fact that we humans try to move toward events, situations, and people that increase our pleasure or reduce our pain. If you feel a need to make a decision but just can't seem to do it, consider the following reasons most people do not make decisions:

- Fear of making mistakes

- Fear of looking foolish

"Sometimes we stare so long at a door that is closing, that we see too late the one that is open."
Thoreau

● Fear of being criticized

● Fear of breaking with family traditions

● Fear of losing security or love

If any of these are you, the decision tools in this chapter will be especially helpful.

Take a look at your decision-making style. How have you made important decisions in the past? What do you usually do when confronted with decisions? Most people's decision-making style fits into one of these descriptions:

1. Wait until someone else makes it for me, assuming they know best.

2. Ask everyone I know what they think, get totally confused, and then decide.

3. Ask one or two people whom I trust and respect and follow their guidance.

4. Do the first thing that comes up, trust it, and work with the results.

5. Worry about it until the day before the deadline and go with what I think at the time.

6. Just wait it out until someone else makes the decision and then go along with it, complaining.

Any of these styles can be effective, though I'm not fond of being around the complaining number six type. Turning to others we trust for advice can yield good results. Frankly, when it was time for me to select a major in college, I turned to an advisor for suggestions. After a brief discussion she told me to major in psychology. That turned out okay for me, but what would have happened if I had stayed with my first selections of economics or history? Who knows? One makes a decision and moves on.

Sometimes I work with clients for whom career seeking is a life-long hobby. Over the years, they never actually change careers, but they go to career counselors every few years to explore their options. In most cases, their dissatisfaction is linked to another part of their life, usually their relationships at home.

It's time for you to pull together all the information you have gathered and make the best decision you can based on your circumstances and the opportunities available to you.

Research into individual personal styles tells us that about half the people in the United States enjoy making decisions. They like to make decisions quickly and without a fuss. These easy decision makers are drawn to occupations where they can be decisive, such as nurse, salesperson, judge, dentist, physician, policeman, attorney, or medical technologist.

The other half of the population wants to wait for one more piece of information, which may be just around the corner, because they want to make a perfect decision. People who enjoy considering all the options and keeping an open mind for a long time are happier in occupations such as journalist, artist, research assistant, actor, psychologist, social scientist, cook, clerical worker, or x-ray technician.

Define Your Decision Style

Directions: To gain insight into the way you prefer to make decisions, complete the following activity.

1. Jot down three decisions you made in the last year, even if they seem like unimportant decisions:

a. _____

b. _____

c. _____

2. Thinking back, did you ask the advice of other people before you made your final decision or did you go for it, trusting your own head or intuition?

_____

3. Did you tell friends and family members what you were probably going to do to get their reaction before you actually committed? Whom? _____

_____

"The strongest principle of growth lies in human choice."
George Eliot

4. How did they react? _____

5. How did their reaction affect your decision?

_____

6. Did you follow the advice you received without thinking, or did you take it all in and then do what you thought best and then defend your decision?

_____

7. Is there anything you want to change about your decision-making process? If so, what?

_____

8. Consider the career or job decision that is your current creative problem to solve and complete the following sentences:

I want to _____ but _____.

I can't _____ because _____.

I don't want to disappoint _____ by _____

_____.

I can gather support by _____.

I would feel more confident about my choice if _____

_____.

What I'm doing to avoid making this decision is _____

_____.

If I decide not to decide then I will feel _____

_____.

If I decide to go for what I want I will feel _____

_____.

The many good outcomes that I will receive from
   making this decision are

_____.

_____.

I have decided to _____.

And I will do it by (when?) _____.

When you say, "I have a problem," you are expressing a feeling of
being out of control of a situation or you are asking for assistance. The
activity you just completed led you to review the reasons you may be
avoiding decisions and helped you to make a commitment at the end of
the activity. Follow through on your commitment to yourself.

Decision Making ABCs

Decision making is very much like the creative process described in
chapter six. In stage A, you work to identify and understand all of the
issues by defining the existing problem situation, deciding what all of
the issues are, and analyzing the situation as a whole. In this case, you completed questionnaires, asked colleagues, friends, and family members for
feedback, conducted library research, contacted people who work in jobs
that sound interesting, and listened to presentations at professional association meetings.

In stage B, you work to find solutions, by first generating ideas, pri-
oritizing potential decisions, and then evaluating them one by one. This
stage correlates to the incubation stage in the creative process. You now
have some career or job possibilities in front of you, and you are probably leaning toward one or two of them. It's time to use your intuitive
powers to put all the data together and brainstorm possibilities to arrive
at new combinations. If you want help with developing and using your
intuitive powers, the practical handbook *Intuition Workout* by Nancy
Rosanoff (Alsan Publishing, Santa Rosa, CA, 1988) is an exceptional
resource.

In stage C, you plan the action to take by examining the impact your
decision will have, planning what actions to take, and then establishing
a process of follow-through on your decision. The rest of this chapter

provides several activities you can use to make your decision. You can complete all of them or select a few. When your choice of direction is made, you will reactivate your networking contact list to secure a job in the field you chose.

To help you think about the variables to consider in making a decision that will lead to job satisfaction, here are the results of a study in which three thousand adults were asked their definition of success and job satisfaction. The report appears in *The Statistical Handbook of Working America* (Detroit, MI: Gale Research, 1995, Charity Anne Dorgan, Editor).

As you can see from the table, for most of the participants in the study, personal satisfaction from doing a good job was the most important incentive value of success.

	This is success to me
Personal satisfaction from doing a good job	52% yes
Earning respect and recognition from others	30% yes
Getting ahead or advancing in job or career	22% yes
Making a good income	21% yes
Feeling my work is important	12% yes
Having control over work content and schedule	6% yes

No matter what you do, you will decide—directly and consciously, or indirectly and unconsciously—to do whatever you end up doing next. I strongly encourage you to think it through, ask for input from others you respect, and then go into your own mind and heart and make a final decision inside yourself. You have to live out the consequences and learn the lessons of whatever road you walk down. One of the joys of being alive is the privilege of making your own decisions, learning from experiences, loving the consequences, and making adjustments as you go.

Your expression of yourself through your work can be a fascinating, exciting, and interesting set of challenges, accomplishments, wins, and losses. Don't let anything stop you. Enjoy the trip. Read the client stories at the end of the chapter to determine how others made their career decicions.

Take time now to complete the analyses on the following pages. For the decision matrix analysis you will need to refer to the exercises you did in chapter three.

A Summary of Me at This Time

1. What I value most highly in a job is:

_____

2. The most important factors of a career are:

_____

3. I want to work around people who have these qualities:

_____

4. I lose track of time when I am doing these activities:

_____

5. My ideal job will reward me for:

_____

6. I leave jobs when:

_____

7. The skills I have used the most in past activities are:

_____

8. The experiences I have had that will contribute the most are:

_____

9. The jobs and careers I am considering now are:

_____

10. My immediate goal is:

_____

11. The job or career that would fulfill my immediate goal is:

_____

12. My long term goal is:

_____

13. The career that would satisfy my long term goal is:

_____

_____

"Integrity without knowelge is weak and useless, and knowedge without integrity is dangerous and dreadful."
Samuel Johnson

Summarize the Information You Have

The worksheets that follow are to help you summarize the information you have to work with. Complete them to help you think through and sort out the data.

Chapter 2 Activity: Personal/Professional Career Survey

Gather the Surveys that were returned to you and summarize the feedback you received.

What did others say your primary interests are?

_____

Which of your abilities do they admire?

_____

What accomplishments do you seem to be proudest of?

_____

What job or career did they say would be a good one for you?

_____

In which of the six categories did they say your strengths lie?

_____

What job or career would you choose if you followed this feedback?

_____

Chapter 3 Activity Summary

Refer back to chapter three to review your responses to the various self-assessment worksheets.

Values Assessment

What are your top five values?

_____

Family Career Script

What careers have you been influenced to choose by family and friends?

_____

Work Preference

What were your number one, two, and three choices?

_____

Personal Style

What were your four preferences?

_____

Degree of Risk Preference

How much risk do you enjoy?

_____

Data People Things Checklist

Which category of activities do you prefer the most strongly?

_____

> "All knowedge is of itself some value. There is nothing so minute or inconsiderable that I would not rather know it than not."
> Samuel Johnson

Chapter 5 Activity

Of the three types of careers described in Chapter Five, the one I want to work in is _____

_____

Chapter 6 Activity

Library Research Results

Summarize the qualities of the three jobs you liked the most when you read about them.

Position Title	Duties and Activities	Rewards	Key points

Chapter 11 Activity

Based on the information interviews you conducted, summarize the positive and unattractive points for each of your top three career choices.

Position title 1. _____

Positive points _____

_____

Unattractive features _____

_____

Position title 2. _____

Positive points _____

_____

Unattractive features _____

_____

Position title 3. _____

Positive points _____

_____

Unattractive features _____

_____

Of these three, my strongest preference is for _____,

even though _____.

The next three activities, the Alternatives Evaluation, Fishbone Diagram, and Force Field Analysis, will help you further refine your thinking and move you closer to making the right decision.

Alternatives Evaluation

Directions: To evaluate three possibilities, list one under Alternative A, B, and C. In the next box over, write down what could go wrong if you choose that alternative. In the next box over, indicate whether those things that could go wrong have a high, mid, or low probability of happening. In the last box, write down how you could avoid or reduce the probability of those events occurring.

Example: If you choose the job five hundred miles away, you may be concerned that you would suffer from being out of contact with friends and family. The probability is determined by you. It could be avoided or reduced through regular telephone contact or planning ahead to get together.

What conclusions can you draw from this exercise?

Alternative A	What could go wrong	Probability: High, Mid, Low	How to avoid or reduce probability
Alternative B	What could go wrong	Probability: High, Mid, Low	How to avoid or reduce probability
Alternative C	What could go wrong	Probability: High, Mid, Low	How to avoid or reduce probability

"It is a most mortifying reflection for a man to consider what he has done compared to what he might have done."
Samuel Johnson

Your Decision Fishbone Diagram

Directions: A fishbone diagram provides a visual of the causes of a problem. In this case you will outline the causes of job dissatisfaction that lead you to look for a new job or career. Job Dissatisfaction is the result of the three problems you list under each of the headings: People (for example: too much contact with the public, personality clash with the management); Tasks/Job Satisfaction (for example: too much repetitive work, want more rewarding work); Work Environment (for example: had to be indoors all the time, dangerous work); and Other (for example, too long a commute, not enough income). Feel free to change or add categories to fully describe your situation.

Step 1. Causes of dissatisfaction with previous employment

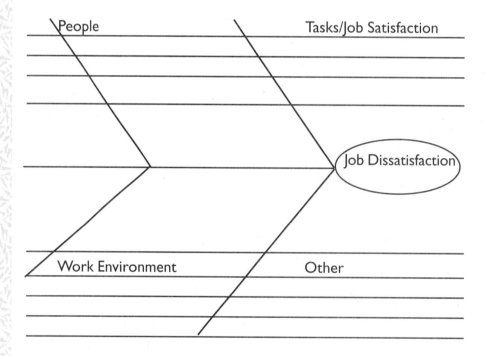

Step 2. Instead of focusing on the causes of a problem, a backward fishbone diagram helps you analyze and compare the consequences of a possible solution. When you use this technique you create a picture of what may result from your decision. In each category, list three results of choosing the new line of work you are currently considering. Feel free to change the titles of the categories to make it more relevant to your situation.

Likely situation if I choose this new line of work

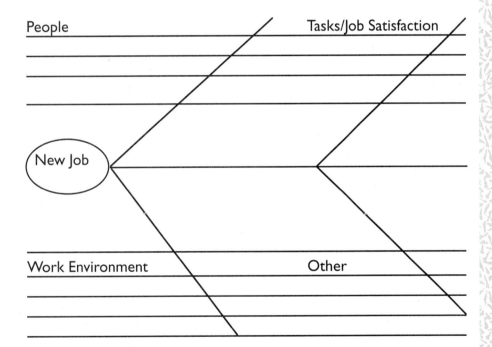

People

Tasks/Job Satisfaction

New Job

Work Environment

Other

Self-confidence is the first requisite to great undertakings."
Samuel Johnson

Force Field Analysis

Directions: Force Field Analysis displays a situation or problem and the positive and negative forces that are influencing your decision. This is a useful method for pulling all of your thoughts together into one diagnostic tool. Review the example below and then complete your own at the bottom of the page.

Example:

Negative Forces			
plenty of routine	physically strenuous	paperwork	
$\downarrow$	$\downarrow$	$\downarrow$	
$\uparrow$	$\uparrow$	$\uparrow$	$\uparrow$
18% growth projected	matches my values	freedom & travel	family supports
Positive Forces			

Idea: Environmental Health Specialist

In this example, the positives outweigh the negatives.

Now complete a Force Field Analysis for your situation.

Negative Forces

Idea: _____

Positive Forces

Decision Matrix

Directions: You will need to refer to the exercises completed earlier in chapter 12 to complete this matrix.

Step 1: Down the left hand column, list the types of work you are considering.

Step 2. In the Decision Tool Column, place a mark if the information you received from each Decision Making Tool indicates that the type of work you listed would be right for you.

Example: If you listed Insurance Underwriter as a Job or Career Possibility, and reviewed the results of the six Decision Tools, you might have an "X" under AE because your completed Alternatives Evaluation indicated that you can overcome the significant What Could Go Wrong possibilities. You put an X in the WP column because your Work Preferences include words such as investigator, technical, systematic, orderly. The PS has an X because Personal Style preferences you listed were Fewer People, Ideas, Efficiency, and Organized. The DRP has an X because your quiz indicated that your Degree of Risk Preference in your work is low - mostly from column B. The FD Fishbone Diagram has an X because you found that most of the previous job dissatisfactions would be absent from the work, and the likely situation would do much to resolve those issues. The FFA has an X because you outlined the Positive and Negative Forces in the Force Field Analysis and found that the positives outweigh the negatives.

Interpretation: The results are fairly simple to evaluate. The Job or Career Possibility with the most X marks is where you should put your efforts. Armed with information, the network you have developed, and clarity that you have made the right decision, you are ready to go forth and get your job.

> "Men must be decided on what they will not do, and then they are able to act with vigor in what they ought to do."
> Mencius

Job or Career Possibility	AE	WP	PS	DRP	FD	FFA
example Insurance Underwriter	X	X	X	X	X	X

(column group heading: Decision Tool Column)

Sample case study

Here is an example of the information gathered by a career seeker, Brett W.

Decision making style: Ask everyone I know, get confused, and then decide.

The most important factors in a career for Brett are: Not to sit at a desk all day and to make enough money to have extra to save.

The ideal job will reward him for: Hard work and helping others.

Brett leaves jobs when: He gets bored.

The careers he is considering are: Ambulance driver, firefighter, and opening his own small engine repair shop.

Brett's immediate goal is: Employment in a career where he has steady work for at least the next few years.

The job or career that would fulfill the immediate goal: ambulance driver and firefighter.

His long term goal is: to live away from the city and raise a family.

Personal/Professional Career Summary

Brett asked six family members and friends to complete surveys. They clearly emphasized Brett's physical orientation to the world. Four of the surveys said that the accomplishments he was proudest of were his work with the rescue patrol club he belongs to. The jobs they recommended for Brett were doctor, ambulance driver, firefighter, and helicopter pilot. The abilities they most admired were his calm under pressure, friendships, and sense of humor.

Values Assessment

Brett's top five values are: adventure, friendship, help others, respect, self-respect.

Family Career Script: Brett's father had a cattle ranch. His mother stayed home with the children when they were young and worked as a teacher's assistant when the children were in high school. One of his aunts is a dietitian, and another aunt is an office manager for a dentist. His mother's father was a missionary physician, and his father's father was a rancher. Brett's first job was helping around the ranch, and during the summers in high school he helped the custodian paint the school. During junior college he worked as a clerk in a drug store.

Work Preference: Number one priority is friends and community, number two is investigator, number three is physical, mechanical.

Personal Style: People, Ideas, Efficiency, and Organized

Degree of Risk Preference: Brett has a high average tolerance for risk.

Data People Things: Serve people, coordinate data, handle equipment, do precise operations, operate machinery

Of the three types of careers discussed in chapter five, Brett is most comfortable with: In-person services

Alternatives Evaluation

When Brett completed the alternatives evaluation he considered the things that could go wrong for each of his three choices. For ambulance driver his concern was emotional burn out from working around human crisis situations. He saw it as a midlevel probability and decided that he could reduce the probability of that happening by taking care of himself.

He thought firefighting had a higher level of physical risk that he could comfortably live with, and, other than continuous training, he couldn't think of ways to reduce the probability of it happening.

Owning his own small engine repair shop had financial risks that were high. He knew he could avoid some of the risk by careful planning, but he wasn't sure it was the right time in his life. (This could become a mid-life or retirement dream that comes true in thirty years.)

Force Field Analysis

This was easy to complete based on the library research and the information interviews. For ambulance driver the Negative Forces were boredom, burn out, and physical danger. The Positive Forces were job growth, matches his values, not sitting at a desk, fits into family career script, respect the job.

The Force Field Analysis for firefighter included on the Negative Forces indoors a lot between firefighting, highly stressful, physical danger. The Positive Forces were job growth, physical job, helping people, and matches his values.

For opening a small engine repair shop the Negative Forces included start-up costs, long hours, being indoors virtually all the time. The Posi-

"Where the willingness is great, the difficulties cannot be great." Machiavelli

"The future is purchased by the present."
Samuel Johnson

tive Forces were helping others, working with equipment and machinery, independence, and an opportunity for high earnings over time.

Which of these three careers would you choose for Brett?

Brett's decision was to move back to the community where grew up and to open a small engine repair shop. The information interviews he conducted convinced him that he would gain the greatest sense of community and respect from others in that setting. He realized that firefighting was too dangerous and that driving an ambulance would not provide the types of relationships he needed to be satisfied. To overcome the negative of being indoors so much of the time, he hired a helper who stayed in the store while he worked in the shop. It reduces his feeling of being confined by the demands of a retail setting. Brett also took the training required and became an Emergency Medical Technician and now volunteers at community events, assisting ambulance drivers.

A Final Note

You are very fortunate to have made a career decision that is based on a solid review of what motivates you, the reality of the job marketplace, and information interviews that revealed the ups and downs of the jobs you considered. Most people you meet feel that they took the job that seemed available at the time and got stuck in it.

As you contact the people in your network to begin a job search and start interviewing, you are building on the experiences you gained through talking with many people on the telephone and in person during this process. If your first job interview does not result in an offer for employment, don't be discouraged. You have proven to yourself that you have what it takes to stick with a project that took considerable self-discipline to complete. Securing a job that uses your talents in an organization where you can make a contribution that is meaningful to you is a goal worth holding out for.

I can predict with certainty that the future that you create for yourself is exactly the one you will live. Whether you choose to stay with your current career, go to school to prepare for a new career, or find a new way to use the skills you already have, I wish you the best of everything that life has to offer.

Bibliography and Resources

The following books are useful, if not indispensable, in learning about jobs, careers, succeeding in the work environment, and life in general. Most of them can be readily found in libraries, career centers, and resource centers. This is not a reading list so much as a browsing and resource list.

General

Boldt, Laurence G. *Zen and the Art of Making a Living: A Practical Guide to Creative Career Design,* rev. ed. (New York: Arkana, 1993). Discusses one path to success.

Bolles, Richard Nelson. *What Color Is Your Parachute?: A Practical Manual for Job-Hunters and Career-Changers* (Berkeley, CA: Ten Speed Press, 1996). The standard manual for job seekers, published annually.

Collard, Betsy A. *The High-Tech Career Book: Finding Your Place in Today's Job Market* (Los Altos, CA: W. Kaufmann, 1986). Includes vocational guidance involving high-technology industries.

Djeddah, Eli. *Moving Up: How to Get High-Salaried Jobs,* new ed. (Berkeley, CA: Ten Speed Press, 1978). Comments on how to move forward financially.

Eikleberry, Carol. *The Career Guide for Creative and Unconventional People* (Berkeley, CA: Ten Speed Press, 1995).

Feingold, S. Norman, and Norma Reno Miller. *Emerging Careers: New Occupations for the Year 2000 and Beyond* (Garrett Park, MD: Garrett Park Press, 1983).

Figler, Howard. *Liberal Education and Careers Today* (Garrett Park, MD: Garrett Park Press, 1989).

Jandt, Fred E., and Mary B. Nemnich. *Using the Internet in Your Job Search* (Indianapolis, IN: JIST Works, 1995). Discusses computer sources as a means to finding a job.

Kennedy, Joyce Lain, and Thomas J. Morrow. *Electronic Job Search Revolution: How to Win with the New Technology That's Reshaping Today's Job Market,* 2nd ed. (New York: J. Wiley, 1995). Provides tips on technological innovations and computer network resources for job searching.

Kennedy, Joyce Lain. *Hook Up, Get Hired!: The Internet Job Search Revolution* (New York: J. Wiley, 1995). Covers job hunting via the internet.

Kennedy, Joyce Lain, and Darryl Laramore. *Joyce Lain Kennedy's Career Book,* 2nd ed. (Lincolnwood, IL: VGM Career Horizons, 1993). Includes vocational guidance and career development advice.

Krannich, Ronald L., and Caryl Rae Krannich. *Jobs & Careers with Nonprofit Organizations* (Manassas Park, VA: Impact Publications, 1996). Lists associations and organizations to help the job-seeker enter into the nonprofit field.

Petras, Kathryn, and Ross Petras. *The Only Job Hunting Guide You'll Ever Need: The Most Comprehensive Guide for Job Hunters and Career Switchers,* updated and rev. (New York: Simon & Schuster, 1995).

Petras, Kathryn, and Ross Petras. *The Over-40 Job Guide* (New York: Poseidon Press, 1993). Helps middle-aged persons find jobs.

Tieger, Paul D., and Barbara Barron-Tieger. *Do What You Are: Discover the Perfect Career for You Through the Secrets of Personality Type,* 2nd ed. (Boston: Little, Brown, 1995). Tries to link a person's personality with the most suitable occupation.

Yate, Martin. *Knock 'em Dead: The Ultimate Job Seeker's Handbook* (Holbrook, MA: Bob Adams, 1996).

Interviewing

Krannich, Caryl Rae, and Ronald Krannich. *Interview for Success: A Practical Guide to Increasing Job Interviews, Offers, and Salaries* (Manassas Park, VA: Impact Publications, 1995).

Medley, H. Anthony. *Sweaty Palms: The Neglected Art of Being Interviewed* (Berkeley, CA: Ten Speed Press, 1993). Discusses everything a person needs to know about interviews and interviewing, from what types of interviews there are to what to wear.

Yate, Martin. *Knock 'em Dead: With Great Answers to Tough Interview Questions* (Holbrook, MA: Bob Adams, 1992).

Networking

Baber, Anne, and Lynne Waymon. *Great Connections: Small Talk and Networking for Businesspeople,* 2nd ed. (Manassas Park, VA: Impact Publications, 1992). Discusses business and interpersonal communications.

Baker, Wayne E. *Networking Smart: How to Build Relationships for Personal and Organizational Success* (New York: McGraw-Hill, 1994). Analyzes communication and how it works within organizations.

Chin-Lee, Cynthia. *It's Who You Know: Career Strategies for Making Effective Personal Contacts* (San Diego, CA: Pfeiffer, 1993). Describes social networks.

Krannich, Ronald L., and Caryl Rae Krannich. *Network Your Way to Job and Career Success: The Complete Guide to Creating New Opportunities* (Manassas Park, VA: Impact Publications, 1989).

McKay, Matthew, Martha Davis, and Patrick Fanning. *Messages: The Communications Skills Book,* 2nd ed. (Oakland, CA: New Harbinger Publications, 1995).

Raye-Johnson, Venda. *Effective Networking* (Los Altos, CA: Crisp Publications, 1990).

RoAne, Susan. *The Secrets of Savvy Networking: How to Make the Best Connections for Business and Personal Best* (New York: Warner Books, 1993). Includes social network and business etiquette information.

Recent Graduates

Bloom, Bruce J. *Fast Track to the Best Job: How to Launch a Successful Career Right Out of College* (Scarsdale, NY: Blazer Books, 1991).

Bouchard, Jerry. *Graduating to the 9-5 World* (Woodbridge, VA: Impact Publications, 1991). Includes interviewing and new employee orientation.

O'Brien, Jack. Kiplinger's *Career Starter: Your Game Plan for a Successful Job Search* (Washington, DC: Kiplinger Books, 1993).

Rowe, Fred A. *The Career Connection: A Guide to College Majors and Their Related Careers,* rev. ed. (Indianapolis, IN: JIST Works, 1991).

Rowe, Fred A. *The Career Connection II: A Guide to Technical Majors and Their Related Careers,* rev. ed. (Indianapolis, IN: JIST Works, 1991).

Career Change

Farr, J. Michael. *The Right Job for You: An Interactive Career Planning Guide* (Indianapolis, IN: JIST Works, 1991). Lists different occupations and provides job application tips.

Kanchier, Carole. *Dare to Change Your Job and Your Life,* rev. ed. (Indianapolis, IN: JIST Works, 1995).

Lauber, Daniel. *Professional's Private Sector Job Finder* (River Forest, IL: Planning Communications, 1994). Gives vocational guidance.

Quittel, Frances. *Fire Power* (Berkeley, CA: Ten Speed Press, 1994). Covers topics such as job security and starting over if you lose your job.

Savino, Carl S., and Ronald L. Krannich. *From Army Green to Corporate Grey: A Career Transition Guide for Army Personnel* (Manassas Park, VA: Impact Publications, 1994). Discusses career options for former Army personnel.

Shingleton, John D., and James Anderson. *Mid-Career Changes: Strategies for Success* (Orange, CA: Career Publishing, 1993). Comprehensive guide aimed at the unemployed or those seeking different employment.

Stevens, Paul. *Stop Postponing the Rest of Your Life* (Berkeley, CA: Ten Speed Press, 1993). Discusses career development.

Resumes & Cover Letters

Good, C. Edward. *Resumes for Re-Entry: A Handbook for Women,* 2nd ed. (Manassas Park, VA: Impact Press, 1993).

Kaplan, Robbie Miller. *Sure-Hire Cover Letters* (New York: AMACOM, 1991).

Kennedy, Joyce Lain, and Thomas J. Morrow. *Electronic Resume Revolution: Creating a Winning Resume for the New World of Job Seeking,* 2nd ed. (New York: J. Wiley, 1995).

Parker, Yana. *The Damn Good Resume Guide,* 3rd ed. (Berkeley, CA: Ten Speed Press, 1996).

Weddle, Peter D. *Electronic Resumes for the New Job Market* (Manassas Park, VA: Impact Publications, 1995).

Yate, Martin. *Cover Letters that Knock 'em Dead,* rev. and expanded (Holbrook, MA: Bob Adams, 1995).

Yate, Martin. *Resumes that Knock 'em Dead,* rev. and expanded (Holbrook, MA: Bob Adams, 1995).

Other

Calvert, Bob, editor. "Career Opportunities News" (Garrett Park, MD: Garrett Park Press). A career information newsletter.

Dictionary of Occupational Titles, 2 vols., 4th ed. (Washington, D.C.: U.S. Department of Labor, Employment, and Training Administration, 1977).

Gottfredson, Gary D., and John L. Holland. *Dictionary of Holland Occupational Codes,* 2nd ed., rev. and expanded (Odessa, FL: Psychological Assessment Resources, 1989).

Guide for Occupational Exploration (Washington, D.C.: U.S. Department of Labor, Employment, and Training Administration, 1979).

Keirsey, David, and Marilyn Bates. *Please Understand Me: Character and Temperament Types,* 5th ed. (Del Mar, CA: Prometheus Nemesis, 1984). Discusses personality and temperament.

Reich, Robert B. *The Work of Nations: Preparing Ourselves for 21st Century Capitalism* (New York: Vintage Books, 1992). Talks about international economic relations and provides economic forecasts.

Self-Esteem

Branden, Nathaniel. *The Six Pillars of Self-Esteem* (New York: Bantam Books, 1994). Includes the basic principles of self-esteem and discusses the external influences that people undergo.

McKay, Matthew, and Patrick Fanning. *Self-Esteem,* 2nd ed. (Oakland, CA: New Harbinger Publications, 1993).